THE INSIDER'S GUIDE TO THE FINANCIAL SERVICES REVOLUTION

Alan Gart, Ph.D.

McGraw-Hill Book Company

New York   St. Louis   San Francisco   Auckland   Bogotá
Hamburg   Johannesburg   London   Madrid   Mexico
Montreal   New Delhi   Panama   Paris   São Paulo
Singapore   Sydney   Tokyo   Toronto

Library of Congress Cataloging in Publication Data

Gart, Alan.
   The insider's guide to the financial services
revolution.

   Includes index.
   1. Financial institutions—United States.
I. Title.   II. Title: Financial services revolution.
HG181.G37   1984   332.1'0973   82–22950
ISBN 0-07-022891-4

1234567890   DOCDOC   89876543

ISBN 0-07-022891-4

The editors for this book were William A. Sabin and Frances Koblin,
the designer was Dennis Sharkey, and the production supervisor was
Teresa F. Leaden. It was set in Compano by The Kingsport Press.

Printed and bound by R. R. Donnelley & Sons Company.

CONTENTS

About the Author

Alan Gart is a professor of finance and international business at Florida International University and president of Alan Gart Inc., an economic and financial consulting company located in Philadelphia, Pennsylvania. A regular participant at numerous conferences, he has served as a consultant for Manufacturers Hanover Trust Company, The Philadelphia Saving Fund Society, INA Capital Advisors, Parkway Management, and CIGNA Corporation, among others. He is a frequent contributor to business and professional journals, book reviews, and monthly economic newsletters. Dr. Gart, who received his Ph.D. from the University of Pennsylvania, has also been a senior vice president at the Girard Bank, a vice president at Manufacturers Hanover Trust Company, and chief economist at INA Corporation.

Preface

Financial institutions have undergone enormous change over the last few years and are likely to change even more during the remainder of the decade. *The Insider's Guide to the Financial Services Revolution* offers rich insights into the problems of financial institutions. It also outlines the direction in which our financial giants are moving and attempts to predict their probable structural outcome.

Changes in technology, distribution systems, and deregulation are among the salient themes unfolding within the financial services industry. Increased competition, merger and acquisition activity, and cross-selling within financial conglomerates are other emerging trends. There also appears to be less customer loyalty in the eighties. If a better deal is offered across the street, many customers will walk away from a bank or an insurance agent where they have done business for many years. Insurance, in particular, has taken on many of the characteristics of a commodity when it comes to consumer price sensitivity.

With the latest deregulation allowing banks and thrifts to offer money market accounts, depository institutions have won some live ammunition to fight off the securities brokerage houses, insurance companies, and money market funds that in recent years invaded what traditionally had been the "banker's turf." It has become more difficult to distinguish differences between the financial services offered to the consumer by brokers, banks, savings and loan associations, money market funds, and insurance companies, especially with the movement toward financial conglomeration.

From the shift in the distribution system in personal lines insurance to the cross-selling of employee benefits and property and casualty coverage at the corporate level, the insurance industry is beginning to change. Change is also occurring rapidly in the banking industry as new depository products are continually being unveiled, along with discount brokerage, a plethora of automated teller machines, computerized banking and shopping at home, and for a few bank holding companies export trade subsidiaries. As they advertise and otherwise generate publicity about their clever new tactics, the big banks accordingly exert pressure on the small banks to follow suit. The small banks' central problem is often the lack of depth and expertise in management or the economies of scale required to successfully play follow the leader. Moreover, as old regulations and restrictions give way, the legislated underpinnings of their profitability could crumble quickly. Despite the big banks' grand strategies, bankers—big and small—often end up doing what they have always done: imitating one another.

Currently, many bankers claim that they are segmenting the market and can no longer be all things to all people. They are seeking a niche, which is probably to attract the high-income customer, who can be "cross-sold" a variety of profitable personal banking services.

The financial services industry has been under great strain over the last few years. Volatile interest rates and double-digit inflation, followed by deflation and a record number of corporate bankruptcies have led to a huge number of bank failures in the United States— the largest number since the great depression. Also, a combination of exceptionally high interest rates, worldwide recession, and declining commodity prices have made it extremely difficult for some developing countries, particularly in Latin America and Eastern Europe to meet their debt service obligations. The fear of a Third World debt default that could trigger a worldwide financial crisis has led to international financial stress. As countries experience strain, the flow of bank credit to certain other countries—freely available only a few months before— has been curtailed, threatening further problems.

The savings and loan associations and the mutual savings banks, with their low-yielding fixed-rate mortgage loans and high-cost deposits, have also had a record number of failures and forced mergers. With lower interest rates and newly granted commercial banking powers, the thrifts will be fighting hard to survive and prosper in the years ahead.

With the huge underwriting losses among our property and casualty insurance companies, there exists the possibility of an insolvency scenario evolving because of the current rate-cutting pattern and the lower interest rates available for investing cash flows. Investment income can no longer offset underwriting losses in some instances. Still, many companies are cutting rates in order to retain or increase their share of the market, theorizing that by remaining competitive during this downward leg of the market cycle, they will be in a better position to do more business when the market cycle turns upward. Although many insurance executives anticipate that some companies will fail, allowing others to eventually sell policies more profitably, many apparently are also convinced that their company will survive and so become participants in cutting premiums. This continued price cutting could produce a vicious cycle that could lead to financial shakeout within the property and casualty insurance industry.

Investment bankers and stockbrokers are also finding competition more severe and profits more difficult to obtain. The investment banking community is attempting to adjust to corporate shelf registrations, which potentially limit the profits on underwriting activity. Commercial banks have also been permitted to sell commercial paper—once the exclusive preserve of the investment banks. The brokerage community faces increased competition from independent discount brokers and discount brokerage operations at banks and at savings and loan associations. The money market funds established at depository institutions will offer increased competition to those available at brokerage firms.

In the past, when interest rates rose substantially, banks and thrifts suffered severe losses of deposits to higher-yielding money market instruments (disintermediation). With losses of deposits, these institutions were forced to cut back on mortgage, consumer, and small-business loans. Usury laws and legislated interest rate ceilings also contributed to this lack of availability of mortgage and consumer credit.

Now that banks and thrifts are permitted to have insured, deregulated money market accounts that can compete with other money market instruments and vehicles, they should no longer suffer massive losses of deposits during periods of high interest rates. Disintermediation at depository institutions may then become a dinosaur. The end of disintermediation would be a blessing for the housing industry, which is dependent upon depository flows into thrifts for mortgage loans. However, variable-rate mortgages and other new mortgage instruments are likely to replace the low-cost fixed-rate mortgage at thrift institutions.

These are just a few examples of the problems and challenges facing the financial intermediaries that are dealt with in this book. Although deregulation helped increase competition and bring down consumer air fares in the travel industry, it was also one of the factors that led to increased financial difficulties and more failures among the airlines. *The Insider's Guide to the Financial Services Revolution* will attempt to answer the question: Will financial deregulation increase the prospect for profits among banks, thrifts, investment banks, and brokerage firms, or will it induce an increase in bankruptcies?

It must be remembered that all these changes in our financial institutions are taking place so rapidly that it is difficult to keep the book up to date. However, I have attempted to include all the changes in regulation and new products and services that were announced prior to December 1982. Every effort has been made to anticipate future change, but as you can imagine, this is a difficult chore.

I have also provided some background information on our financial institutions in an effort to give the reader a better understanding of how some of these financial services have evolved. A glossary of terms, italicized in the text for easy reference, is also included to assist the reader.

Acknowledgments

Writing a first book is a semipainful experience, but it is at the same time an enlightening and pleasant experience. Not only do you acquire new perspectives and insights into your subject matter, but you learn a great deal about yourself.

I wish to thank my family for their understanding, patience, and cooperation. I apologize to my children, Lisa and Steven, and to my wife, Deedy, for the lack of attention they received and for tolerating my many moods during this endeavor. I also want to thank my parents, Herman and Zelda Gart, for their encouragement and love over the years. Dina Oddis, Toni Impriano, Cheryl Stark, Naomi Siegel, and Zelda, Deedy, and Steven Gart all deserve a note of thanks in helping to type and retype various versions of the book.

I sincerely appreciate valuable comments, criticisms, and suggestions made by Walter Hoadley (Bank of America and the Hoover Institute), Jack Lavery (Merrill Lynch), David Melnicoff (PSFS), Edward I. Altman (NYU), Jean McIntosh (Fidelity Bank), Mike Melloy (First Pennsylvania Bank), John Burd (Parkway Management), Jerry D. Belloit and Gus Treichel (FIU), Rick Lang and Deborah McNaulty (Federal Reserve Bank of Philadelphia), and Saul Klaman (National Association of Mutual Savings Banks). Kiril Sokoloff, a consultant to McGraw-Hill, became an invaluable critic. Also, it has been an exceptionally pleasant experience to work with Bill Sabin and with Frances Koblin of McGraw-Hill.

Alan Gart

Most observers will readily agree that many major changes are occurring within our financial institu-

INTRODUCTION

tions. During 1982, more than 40 commercial banks and mutual savings banks failed. That was more than twice the postwar peak of 16 failures which occurred during 1976. In the second quarter of 1982, both Continental Illinois and Chase Manhattan reported losses, the first time since World War II that any of the top 10 banks in this country lost money.

The number of banks on the problem list at the FDIC had risen to about 320 in October from about 220 in January 1982. This list is expected to expand over the next year and surpass in number the 385 banks that were on the FDIC's list following the last major recession in 1976. Many analysts predict a sharp increase in the number of loan losses and in nonperforming loans during 1983. Even though the decline in inflation and interest rates are expected to improve the economy, banking problems tend to lag behind problems in the economy, so that many of the more serious problems in bank loans will be faced during 1983 and 1984.

The *thrift institutions* are hovering on insolvency. *Money market funds,* which did not even exist as an industry in 1973, hold over $223 billion in assets, as of this writing. The low-cost *fixed-rate mortgage*—the hallmark of the postwar period—has now become a dinosaur, and *variable-rate mortgages* are the order of the day. With the drying up of funds in the mortgage market and the rise of mortgage rates to unprecedented levels, the housing industry has suffered its worst downturn in the postwar period. A host of new products have come along for consumers:

24-hour banking through automated tellers, *All Savers certificates, NOW accounts,* 6-, 30-, and 42-month savings certificates, and money market accounts, to name just a few.

These events are more than just the normal evolution of financial services. We would argue that what we are seeing is actually a revolution, with enormous implications to everyone involved in the industry. This book has been written to describe exactly what has happened so far and what is likely to happen in the future. We will discuss the likely effects of the revolution on our major financial institutions—banks, savings and loan associations, insurance companies, and investment banks—and on those who are employed in the industry. The upcoming changes will be both violent and profound. The old, staid world of banking, with stability and job security has now changed to a dangerous game of frequent checkmate. It is probably safe to say that employees in the financial services industry will be affected by the forthcoming changes to a greater degree than at any time in the last 50 years. The key to survival for the institutions and for individuals involved in the industry will be a clear understanding of what is happening. In the new competitive environment that we foresee, change may be so rapid that an institution or employee may have to make an important decision in an unnervingly short period of time. Having a vision of the future and a strategy for survival could aid enormously in adapting to these difficult times.

When the financial historians sit down to write about this revolution, they will probably start their discussion with the acceleration in the rate of inflation which began in the early 1970s. When Richard Nixon closed the gold window in 1971, and the world entered a period of freely fluctuating currencies, the handwriting was on the wall: There was no longer any restraint on the U.S. government's inflationary tendencies. A few visionaries foresaw what would happen, but the events of the 1970s came as a total surprise to most financial experts because there was no recent precedent for it in this country.

One farseeing individual was Bruce Bent of The Reserve Fund, formerly a money market expert at a major insurance company in New York. Bent saw the opportunities in an inflationary environment, that interest rates would rise and that savers would look for a haven for their funds that would protect capital. Accordingly, Bent and a partner began The Reserve Fund in 1971, which, to our knowledge, was the first money market fund to come into existence. In retrospect, the decision to start that fund deserves more than a footnote in financial history because it altered the whole financial services industry in a profound way.

The advantage of money market funds, and why they grew faster than any other industry in the history of finance, was that they could operate outside of the regulation which restrained the banking industry. The nature of this regulation will be discussed more fully in the text, but suffice it to say here that under *Regulation Q*, the interest rate that banks and thrift institutions could pay on deposits was restricted. That proved to be an enormous impediment to these financial institutions in an era of rapidly rising rates and a growing fear of double-digit inflation among the populace.

The money funds, with average maturities in their portfolios of between, say, 15 and 40 days, depending on their prediction of the direction of interest rates, could quickly reflect an increase in interest rates. Anyone who bought an extended-maturity savings certificate from a bank between 1977 and 1980 regretted it quickly, as interest rates continued to rise. Money funds were quick to capitalize on this advantage, pointing out that they offered instant liquidity and a hedge against inflation and interest rate volatility. Later, as the industry really began to grow, the funds provided free check-writing services for checks over $500. Thus, you were able to get a checking account free of transaction charges which paid you interest while the check was waiting to clear. It is not hard to see why money funds have been such formidable competitors for the banks and thrifts.

Nevertheless, to the extent they could, the banks and savings and loan institutions responded with competitive products, and in their own way their efforts were quite successful. The 6-month, 30-month, and other consumer certificates garnered $448 billion worth of deposits by the end of 1981—almost double the amount in checking accounts and up from zero in 1975. Of course, the flip side of this situation was the fact that the banks' cost of funds rose substantially. Instead of getting deposits through checking accounts with no interest costs and through low-cost passbook accounts, the banks found that their cost of funds had doubled. The savings banks and savings and loan associations were in even worse shape because they had made a huge number of fixed-rate mortgages and were locked into a return on their assets that was way below their cost of funds. In October 1982, Congress took a major step toward deregulation by passing a law allowing banks and thrift institutions to offer an account without an interest rate ceiling which would be equivalent to a money market fund account.

Meanwhile, life insurance companies were also hit by the surge in interest rates. A return on cash-value life insurance of only about 4 percent did not seem to make sense to most people. As a result, consumers are now tending to buy pure term insurance; universal life, which pays competitive interest rates on the cash value buildup; or annuities, which also reflect current interest rate levels. Another problem facing the insurance companies was that their policyholders could borrow against the cash value buildup at interest rates of only 5 to 8 percent, depending on when the policy was written. With money market rates vastly in excess of that, policyholders had considerable incentive to borrow against that buildup and put the proceeds in the money market, thereby netting a favorable spread. These policy loans have been an enormous drain on the industry, and coupled with the operating losses in the property and casualty end of the business, little cash flow was left for investments.

What does the future hold? We will focus a good portion of this book on how we think events will unfold, but let us briefly make some broad generalizations about the future:

1. Technology will have an enormous impact on the whole financial services industry. Because of the increased cost of doing business and because of increased competition, banks will use automation to reduce costs. Branch banking, as we have come to know it, will change. In the future, we will be more apt to do our banking via *automated teller machines (ATMs)*, over the phone, or by electronic means. Thus, investments in bricks and mortar will not prove useful in the banking industry's fight for survival. In all probability, the key will be how quickly and effectively the banks adapt and exploit the new technologies to attract and hold business and to reduce operational costs.

2. There will be a fundamental change in the structure of our financial institutions. By the time the revolution is complete, we will probably have a relatively small number of financial conglomerates that will be nearly identical in the services they offer. It will be difficult to differentiate between the ultimate survivors such as Citicorp, Sears, Prudential, and Merrill Lynch. Of course, there will be room, as always, for the specialized "financial boutique" that manages to find a profitable niche for itself. We will discuss later exactly what type of boutiques are most likely to do well, but as an analogy we can recall the host of small computer companies that survived and prospered despite IBM's marketing muscle and financial strength. In one sense, the boutique market should be small enough so that the conglomerates would have no interest in it; or, alternatively, its service should be so specialized that a mass market would not be equipped to handle the business.

3. The financial environment has changed dramatically—from one of bailouts to one of self-sufficiency. For most of the postwar period, borrowers and lenders were confident that the government and/or the Federal Reserve would bail them out of imprudent or

wrongful decisions. As a result, excesses in the financial arena were allowed to take place which would never have been permitted in another era. The problem loans at the banks, the Drysdale Securities fiasco, the failure of Lombard-Wall Inc., and the bankruptcies of Penn Square and United American Bank are bringing home to the banks the glaring truth that healthy growth is one thing but bad loans are something totally different. The highest real interest rates since the 1930s and the pain of trying to end inflation is also bringing home to a lot of borrowers the two-edged sword of leverage. It is probable that the net result of this traumatic experience will be new prudence in the borrowing and lending process.

4. The phasing out of Regulation Q will allow the banks to compete effectively against the money funds. In fact, one could argue that the money funds will have to scramble hard to come up with services that they can offer more effectively than the banks, now that their interest rate advantage has disappeared. This is especially so since banks can now offer their depositors insurance coverage, which many money funds do not have.

5. Because of a higher cost of funds, banks will likely emphasize the generation of fee income, as against asset-based income. Put another way, assets will "flow" through a bank, with the bank keeping a small spread or piece of the action for itself. Further, the volatility of interest rates will make banks increasingly cautious about taking any sort of interest rate risk. The stakes are just too great if a bank is in error in its interest rate forecast. Thus, banks will operate on the basis of a spread—loans will be offered at a fixed percentage above their cost of funds.

6. Acquisitions of existing financial institutions may not be the way to go. If bricks and mortar become less important and advertising assumes a greater role in garnering consumer deposits, a sleepy financial institution may not be worth what many acquiring institutions are currently paying. Nevertheless, an enormous consolidation will continue in the industry, as financial institutions try to reduce their operating costs by spreading the business over a larger and larger base.

7. Employees in this industry must recognize that the old days of security and stability are over. We are in unprecedented times, with consolidations, failures, and huge market-share shifts the order of the day. One must adapt to this new environment in order to survive.

The financial revolution also encompasses a lot of other areas. On the whole, our goal in this book is to cover the gamut of our financial intermediaries: commercial banks, savings and loan associations, mutual savings banks, credit unions, mutual funds, money market funds, and life, health, property, and casualty insurance companies.

The first chapter, Current Trends in Financial Services, examines the changes taking place within the financial services industry, as well as the regulatory framework and evolution of a system of specialized financial institutions. Recent legislative reforms and an array of innovations have altered the competitive relationship among financial intermediaries in the attempt to provide consumer financial services. Services once exclusively provided by commercial banks are now offered by mutual savings banks, savings and loan associations, credit unions, investment companies, brokerage firms, and even some large retailers. Two extreme polarities in the changing structure of financial institutions are explored: the financial boutique and the financial supermarket.

Chapter two, Banking's Historical Structures, Regulation, and Current Evolution, explores the current banking structure, the growth of financial conglomerates, NOW accounts, money market funds, interstate banking, the problems of our failing thrift institutions, Regulations Q and D, and restrictive legislation such as *Douglas, Glass-Steagall,* and *McFadden,* as well as the less restrictive bank holding company legislation.

Chapter three, The Financial Conglomerates, examines the role of Merrill Lynch, Sears, American Express, and Prudential within the financial services industry. It suggests that this industry will be considerably less fragmented in the future and that the industry will most likely be composed of huge institutions, the largest of which will offer a complete spectrum of banking, insurance, and other financial services.

Chapter four, Retail Commercial Banking, defines the market for consumer financial services. It discusses the battle between commercial banks, money market funds, and thrift institutions for consumer deposits. The role of *electronic funds transfer systems (EFTS)* and the lack of profit in retail banking at most commercial banks are carefully analyzed.

Chapter five, Thrift Institutions and Credit Unions, examines the battle for survival of savings and loan associations and mutual savings banks. The role of thrift institutions in the consumer mortgage market is carefully explored, as are the new mortgage instruments. The role of credit unions and IRAs in the consumer financial revolution are also examined.

Wholesale Banking, Chapter six, is concerned with loans to domestic corporations, multinational companies, governmental agencies, supranational institutions, and small and midsized businesses and the associated deposit relationships. The wholesale market is now and always has been a national or international market. There are no geographic restrictions. The visible trends in the servicing of the credit needs of the wholesale customer are examined, as is the competition for domestic business between U.S. commercial banks and both foreign banks and the commercial paper market. Companies such as General Electric Credit and some of the insurance giants have proved to be tough competitors for many of the nation's commercial banks in the battle for corporate loans. The use of the futures market to hedge interest rate risks, the concept of deintermediation, and the development of nonasset sources of income are carefully explored. The Eurocurrency and Asiacurrency markets and the international political and banking mechanism are introduced. Although U.S. banks have lost market share, and their dominance of the Euroloan syndication market has slipped, they still remain an important factor in the wholesale Eurodollar market. The role of international banking facilities in this country, new international developments such as worldwide money market funds, the diversification of pension funds into international markets, and the competition between foreign banks and United States commercial banks in this country and abroad are examined.

Chapter seven, Investment Banking and Brokerage, is concerned with such changes in this financial sector as the development of discount brokers and negotiated rates for institutional business, the recent acquisition of brokerage firms by financial conglomerates, as well as changes in the sources of income to investment banking firms. There has been a constant innovation of new products and services arising from insurance offerings, lease financing, real estate, options, commodities, money market funds, zero-coupon discount bonds, and the creative aspects of extensive merger and acquisition activity.

Chapter eight, Mutual Funds, examines the impact of money market firms on the financial services industry and the money and capital markets. The development of money market funds has dramatically changed the face of retail banking and consumer investment behavior.

The concept of insurance is traced from its origins to recent developments in Chapter nine, Insurance. The investment role of the insurance industry in the money and capital markets is explored. The purchase of stock brokerage firms by some of the major insurers could potentially lead to a change in the distribution system for insurance sales, with mass marketing becoming an even more important method of selling insurance. It is likely that insurance, as well as other financial services, will be available for sale in the home, or even at bank branches. It is expected that the way we market goods and services could change dramatically because of the home computer. Competitive price information from the cost of automobiles to the cost of bank loans or insurance may be available on our home computer–TV screens before too long. The consumer will have the option of paying for these products and services by using a credit card or debit card.

The final chapter, Implications of the Financial Services Revolution, discusses the details surrounding the financial revolution and suggests the most likely course of events that will develop. It explores ways in which financial institutions and their employees can survive and even profit from the financial revolution. It also covers the implications of all these developments for the ultimate beneficiary of competition—the consumer.

In addition, we will attempt to answer the following questions:

☐ What is the financial revolution? How will it affect our lives? What can we do about it? How can you become a more intelligent and sophisticated observer and investor?
☐ Will the interstate mergers among thrift institutions lead to interstate branch banking?
☐ How many thrift institutions will actually fail?
☐ Will hedging in the futures market protect thrifts and commercial banks against interest rate risks?
☐ Do banks really have enough capital to expand nationally? Will the financial revolution lead to one-stop financial shopping, i.e., the development of financial services supermarkets?
☐ Will the regulatory authorities permit the European concept of the "universal bank" to be adopted in the United States?
☐ Will Sears, Prudential, and American Express really benefit from the cross-selling opportunities now available through their recent brokerage acquisitions?
☐ What will be the impact of electronic banking on the consumer, on interstate banking, on the "bricks and mortar" concept of branch banking?
☐ What is the possibility of an investor flight from either the commercial paper market or money market funds?
☐ Are our investments in money market funds and our deposits in banks and thrift institutions safe?
☐ Will mortgage rates return to normal interest rate levels?
☐ Will franchising and networking become more important?
☐ Will consortia of large regional banks be formed to compete with large money center banks?
☐ Will the small independent bank survive? If so, why?
☐ What kind of specialized financial boutique will be most successful?
☐ Will discount brokers continue to penetrate the retail market for stock brokerage commissions?

- Will the distribution system for the sale of personal lines of insurance change dramatically over the next few years?
- Will we be able to bank or to buy insurance, cars, and other products and services from our home computer–television system; and, if so, when?
- Will group insurance packages continue to expand for individuals as part of their fringe benefits?
- Will commercial insurance packages continue to expand?
- Will life insurance companies be endangered by the heavy demand for policy loans, the potential losses in their investment bond portfolios, and the slowdown in premium growth associated with the recession? Will the heavy losses expected by property and liability insurers lead to bankruptcies?

Any forecast of the future must take into account the possibility of a delay or a crisis that might circumvent the normal pattern of development. In this regard, it is very important to emphasize the risk of a financial crisis. The interest rate increases we spoke of earlier can also be seen in another light—they are eloquent testimony to the enormous liquidity of our financial and business system. At this writing there are a number of worrisome cracks in that system that may lead to serious financial problems. We have already spoken of some of the problems at the thrifts, at the banks, and in the housing industry, but perhaps a greater danger is another slump in the economy which would accelerate bankruptcies. Such a slump, then, could increase caution among banks and among investors who provide funds to the banks and corporations via certificates of deposit and commercial paper. After the Penn Central default, the commercial paper market shrank by 20 percent. If that were to happen today, there would be a runoff of nearly $35 billion. The money market funds hold nearly one-third of all outstanding commercial paper and any problems in the paper market could spill over into the funds, as unsophisticated shareholders cause a redemption stampede. No one can know the exact magnitude of the risks of a financial crisis, but one should evaluate all aspects of the financial revolution in light of such an eventuality.

For instance, close tabs should be kept on:

- The underlying weakness of the financial system and the risk of collapse
- The inadequate capital of banks and the threat of a run on the commercial paper market and, by implication, money market funds
- The deteriorating credit quality and lack of liquidity of the corporate sector, municipalities, and third-world countries

- A huge increase in the level of policy loans at life insurance companies
- A combined ratio (adding the loss ratio and the expense ratio) of property and liability companies approaching 120, which could lead to the possibility of failures of insurance companies
- The speculation on interest rates by major financial institutions
- The difficulty in financing the government deficit and the "crowding out" effect (denial of credit) on the business sector in meeting its external financing needs in the money and capital markets by the huge borrowing needs of the federal government and its agencies

CHAPTER ONE

CURRENT TRENDS IN FINANCIAL SERVICES

The structure of the financial services industry is in a period of enormous flux. Previously regulated industries are becoming deregulated, in fact, if not in law. Separation of powers or products, which began in the aftermath of the Depression, are now ending and the resulting free-for-all will change the face of the industry.

Let us start by defining what we mean by the financial services industry. Basically, it can be defined as those firms or divisions of companies in the business of lending money, accepting deposits, providing insurance, managing money, creating markets, selling securities, and transferring funds. The major financial intermediaries that make up the financial services industry include *commercial banks, savings and loan associations,* life insurance companies, private pension funds, state and local government employee retirement funds, property and liability insurance companies, *finance companies, mutual savings banks,* money market mutual funds, *credit unions, open-end investment companies* (mutual funds), security brokers and dealers, and investment bankers.

How do they rank according to size? Commercial banks are the largest financial intermediaries from the standpoint of financial assets. Savings and loan associations and life insurance companies follow in distant second and third places. However, if the financial assets of property and casualty insurance companies were added to those of the life insurance companies, the insurance industry would supplant the savings and loan industry in second place. As discussed earlier, money market mutual funds represent the fastest growing members of the financial services industry and have passed mutual savings banks, credit unions, mutual funds, and security brokers and dealers in terms of total financial assets. Table 1-1, which follows, helps place into perspective the size of the various financial intermediaries and their growth patterns over the past two decades.

The primary impact of inflation on depository institutions has been on the cost of acquiring retail deposits and on the loss of customer deposits to money market funds and other financial instruments. Money market funds would not have grown so rapidly if double-digit inflation had not raised money market fund rates significantly above the maximum rates that depository institutions were permitted to pay under Regulation Q. Inflation has further led to the avoidance of fixed-rate, long-term maturity commitments and to the shortening of the maturity structure of the financial markets.[1] It has also led to the temporary collapse of the bond market and refuge in short-term debt by weak companies.

TABLE 1-1
TOTAL ASSETS OF FINANCIAL INTERMEDIARIES AT YEAR-END, 1960–1981 (IN BILLIONS OF DOLLARS)

FINANCIAL INTERMEDIARY	1960	1970	1980	1981
Commercial banks	228.3	504.9	1386.3	1516.6
Savings and loan associations	71.5	176.2	629.8	662.3
Life insurance companies	115.8	200.9	469.8	506.6
Private pension funds	38.1	110.4	286.8	295.8
Finance companies	27.6	64.0	198.6	224.6
State and local government employee retirement funds	22.3	60.3	198.1	222.1
Other insurance companies	26.2	49.9	180.1	194.5
Money market mutual funds	—	—	74.4	181.9
Mutual savings banks	41.0	79.3	171.5	175.5
Credit unions	7.1	18.0	69.2	73.3
Open-end investment companies (mutual funds)	—	46.8	63.7	61.5
Security brokers and dealers	6.7	16.2	33.5	38.5
Real estate investment trusts (REITs)	—	0.9	5.9	5.9

SOURCE: Flow of Funds Accounts: Federal Reserve

TABLE 1-2
INITIAL FOCUS OF FINANCIAL INSTITUTIONS

FINANCIAL INSTITUTIONS	SOURCE OF FUNDS	USE OF FUNDS
Commercial banks	Demand and savings deposits	Commercial, industrial, agricultural loans
Thrift institutions	Consumer savings	Home mortgage loans
Finance companies	Public markets	Consumer and commercial loans
Credit unions	Member deposits	Member loans
Insurance companies	Premiums for life, fire, health, and liability coverage	Insurance losses, investments

The record high and volatile interest rates generated by inflation have left the older order in shambles, for example, the virtual bankruptcy of thrift institutions and the loss of a significant share of the transaction account market (checking accounts) by commercial banks to money market funds. Thus, the deregulation of the market is no longer waiting for legal deregulation.[2]

An elaborate framework of federal and state regulations was passed in the wake of the Great Depression to establish and maintain a system of specialized financial institutions. These institutions were differentiated by product lines and markets (see Table 1-2). Market entry was restricted, geographical location and product lines were limited, and the price of services offered were in some instances controlled. Depository institutions such as banks were provided deposit insurance, but they had controls on what they could pay for funds (Regulation Q). There was also a restriction on competition, as security dealers and investment firms were allowed to provide services which other financial institutions could not offer, and vice versa. For example, commercial banks could not underwrite corporate bonds, while securities dealers and brokers could not accept deposits. These regulations were considered acceptable and desirable by banks, thrift institutions, the government, and the public when they were implemented. However, many of these regulations and restrictions are now outmoded, superfluous, and, in some cases, destructive. Today's financial conglomerates seem to erode the justification for this system of specialized institutions and their regulatory framework.

Commercial banks in the United States had traditionally been distinguished from other financial institutions by their unique *demand deposit* function. However, this, at best, is a technical distinction today, as

TABLE 1-3

GROWTH OF INTEREST-BEARING CHECKING ACCOUNTS AND MONEY MARKET FUNDS AND CERTIFICATES, COMPARED WITH DEMAND DEPOSITS, 1975–1981

	YEAR-END, BILLIONS OF DOLLARS		
	1975	1980	1981
Demand deposits	220.8	275.4	235.0
Interest-bearing checking accounts	1.6	28.3	77.0
Money market funds	3.6	75.8	183.0
Money market certificates	—	412.0	448.0

SOURCE: *Federal Reserve Bulletin*, April 1982.

many money substitutes have exhibited rapid growth over the last decade at both *depository* and *nondepository financial institutions* (see Table 1-3). The net effect has been the development of check-writing privileges in the form of interest-earning NOW accounts at thrift institutions and drafts at money market funds. The money market certificates that commercial banks and thrift institutions began to offer in 1978 represented another important structural change. While *disintermediation* is the process of depository institutions losing funds to marketable instruments, *reintermediation* is defined as a process of deposit mix change within a particular institution from demand, NOW and savings accounts to more interest-sensitive and higher-yielding money market certificate accounts.

The net effect has been the blurring of the distinctions between and among depository and nondepository institutions. Another consequence has been that it has been increasingly difficult for the *central bank* to define money and to impose effective monetary policy.[3]

The financial depository system of the last few decades which consisted of 14,000 commercial banks, 23,000 credit unions, over 4000 savings and loan associations, and 450 mutual savings banks (see Figure 1-1) with an intricate system of regulatory devices and subsidies was built on a set of assumptions that are no longer tenable. These assumptions are related to spatial and functional market separation, government deposit insurance, interest rates ceilings on deposits, and the efficacy of regulatory entry restrictions. The smoothly functioning banking system began to unravel under escalating and volatile interest

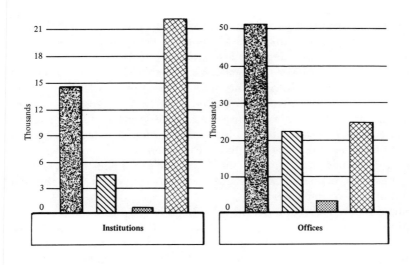

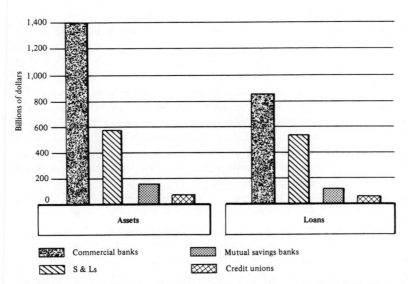

FIGURE 1-1 The competitive lineup in U.S. finance. (*Reprinted from the November 17, 1980, issue of Business Week by special permission, © 1980 by McGraw-Hill, Inc., New York, NY 10020. All rights reserved.*)

rates, highly competitive money market funds, and structural changes in depository ceilings (that greatly impacted thrift institutions) which made traditional bank deposits less attractive to consumers and business. Extremely explosive interest rates and a shift toward higher cost deposits forced banks into liability management and made them reliant upon the money markets. Banks began to retreat from fixed-rate loans and commitments, acknowledging their unwillingness to sustain interest rate risk. The variable-rate loan commitment shifted the risk of variations in market rates of interest to the borrower. Banks with the majority of their assets in fixed-rate loans suffered losses because bank earnings were of longer term maturity and lower return than the cost and maturity of liabilities.[4]

The financial services industry is in the midst of a dramatic transformation. Technological innovations combined with regulatory constraints on depository institutions have enabled nondepository institutions (NDIs) such as Sears, American Express, and Merrill Lynch to make large inroads into markets that have traditionally been the domain of the commercial banks and thrift institutions. This trend is likely to continue and may even accelerate if changes are not made in the regulatory climate. The recent interstate mergers of failing thrift institutions could act as a catalyst in speeding up legislative change that would allow nationwide branch banking.

In addition to the development of money market mutual funds by NDIs, other innovations include asset management services, new cash management techniques and accounts, as well as new financial instruments. Moreover, some financial conglomerates have already formed financial supermarkets or variety stores, offering an array of financial services to customers that are designed to meet the total financial needs of consumers with one-stop shopping.

The likely response to these changes, according to Arnold W. Sametz of The Graduate School of Business of New York University, is "the establishment of specialized financial boutiques and giant multi-purpose financial department and variety stores, which seem to characterize two extreme polarities in the structure of financial institutions."[5] In the former case we have seen the establishment of pure *discount brokerage* firms, strict research shops selling advice for a fee, and specialists in *options* or *reinsurance*. The response to the increased pace of change and risk is not to diversify, but to strip down and unbundle financial services by offering a highly specialized service, product, or function.

At the other extreme, the use of the *bank holding company* umbrella enabled commercial banks to evolve toward the European concept of "universal" banking—the selling of all financial services through a single intermediary. Banks became involved in leasing, some forms of insurance, data processing, financial and economic consulting, and investment banking activity such as merger and acquisition consultation, private placements, offerings of comingled trust funds to the public and the underwriting of municipal revenue bonds. Moreover, brokerage firms began to offer money market funds and insurance to customers. Insurance companies added to their collection of financial services money market funds, annuity packages, brokerage firms, increased term lending to business, real estate, property management, and private placements. Diversification and asset acquisition have been the reaction of many large firms toward the changing financial risks and needs of businesses and consumers, as the concept of one-stop shopping and financial conglomerates have become a reality.

Only a handful of banks can hope to become financial supermarkets. Both large money center and regional banks are seeking strategies that will enable them to find specialities and market niches in which they can compete and grow profitably. They are creating innovative products, developing more sophisticated marketing and operational skills, and consorting with money market funds, brokerage firms, and insurance companies to develop fee-generating services. For example, Bank of America has purchased discount broker Charles Schwab & Company. Provident National Bank in Philadelphia (now merged with Pittsburgh National Corporation to form PNC) has made a niche for itself in selling investment management services to asset management accounts of money market funds of brokerage firms and insurance companies. Columbus-based Banc One Corporation does processing work for Merrill Lynch's *Cash Management Account* (*CMA*), as well as similar work for seven other brokerage firms. Banc One is also negotiating with real estate firms and insurance companies to start a program that would permit customers to borrow against the equity in their homes and life insurance policies via bank cards. State Street Bank and Trust of Boston and Bank of New York process mutual fund and money market fund business. European-American Bank provides analyses of and data on 2100 foreign banks in 118 countries. First Interstate Bancorporation is planning to franchise its name and services nationwide, allowing a bank to remain independent, but offering to it advanced technology, new products, and services for a fee.

A possible configuration or classification of the emerging structural change in U.S. financial systems in the 1980s is offered by James H. Wooden, vice president and financial services industry analyst with Merrill Lynch. He suggested that there might be five categories of financial institutions:[6]

☐ National nonbank, primarily retail-oriented, financial service firms

TABLE 1-4
COMPARISON OF FINANCIAL CONGLOMERATES, IN MILLIONS OF DOLLARS (1981)

COMPARATIVE STATISTICS	AMERICAN EXPRESS	CITICORP	MERRILL LYNCH	PRU-DENTIAL	SEARS
Revenues	7,211	18,375	4,038	14,561	27,357
Net income	518	531	203	NC*	650
Assets	25,103	121,158	17,682	71,564	34,509
Money market funds	15,384	—	45,141	5,312	11,321
Services offered					
Cash management services	X	X	X	X	X
Commercial and residential real estate brokerage			X		X
Commodities brokerage	X		X	X	X
Credit cards, charge cards	X	X	X	X	X
Data processing services	X	X	X		
Executive relocation services			X		X
Foreign exchange trading	X	X	X	X	X
International commercial banking	X	X	X		
International corporate underwriting	X	X	X	X	X
Investment management	X	X	X	X	X
Leasing	X	X	X	X	
Life insurance, health insurance	X		X	X	X
Mortgage banking	X	X	X		X
Mortgage insurance				X	X
Property and casualty insurance	X			X	X
Real estate development				X	X
Savings and loan operations		X			X
Securities brokerage & trading	X	X	X	X	X
Small loan offices		X			X
Traveler's checks	X	X			
U.S. commercial banking		X			X
U.S. corporate underwriting	X		X	X	X

* Not comparable.

that would include, for example, American Express, Prudential, and Sears.
□ National banks with heavy emphasis on technologically based management and product delivery systems that would include, for example, Bank of America, Citicorp, Chase Manhattan, and First Interstate Bancorp.
□ Mostly wholesale commercial banks that perhaps might involve combinations with investment banks should the Glass-Steagall Act change. This would include Morgan Guaranty, Bankers Trust, Continental Illinois, First Chicago, Northern Trust, and Harris Trust.
□ Strong regional or semiregional holding companies, quite possibly including savings and loans as part of them. These would serve the retail and midsized corporate market and would be consolidated units in terms of management structure with a regional base. These might include PNC, PSFS, NCNB, Texas Commerce Bankshares, other strong regional banks, and consortia of regional banks.
□ Boutiques and other specialized institutions and select thrift institutions.

The characteristics of the institutions vary greatly from national firms such as Merrill Lynch, American Express, and Sears (see Table 1-4) to single-office firms such as industrial banks or money market funds. The offer of a postage-free envelope, a free 800 telephone number, and money market yields and liquidity have drawn a considerable amount of savings and checking business away from the traditional depository institutions. Many consumers have learned that it is convenient and cost-effective to obtain financial services from nonlocal institutions.

To place the current situation into the proper framework, it is necessary to consider historical perspective. Since the banks are the largest member of the financial services industry, let us start with them first.

NOTES

1 J. H. Wooden, "Banking Industry: Financial Structural Change Monitor," Merrill Lynch, April–May 1982, p. 7.

2 G. G. Kaufmann, "The Changing Competitive Environment," *Proceedings on the Future of the Financial Services Industry,* Federal Reserve Bank of Atlanta, 1981, p. 90.

3 H. Kaufman, "Banking in the Changing World Credit Markets," *Symposium on a Challenging Future for Banking,* Luxembourg, November 1981, pp. 7–8.

4 S. I. Greenbaum, "Banking in the Next Decade," *The American Banker,* May 29, 1980, p. 4.

5 A. W. Sametz, "The New Financial Environment," *Financial Handbook,* 5th ed., E. I. Altman, John Wiley & Sons, New York, 1981, p. 1.8–1.11.

6 J. H. Wooden, pp. 9–10.

CHAPTER

TWO

BANKING'S HISTORICAL STRUCTURE, REGULATION, AND CURRENT EVOLUTION

STRUCTURE It is important to explore the present regulatory climate which limits bank activity and the regulatory authorities which supervise this activity. After such an exploration, one can see how our financial institutions have circumvented some regulations and how the existing structure of banking is beginning to change. We will examine what might happen when depository interest rate ceilings are eliminated and which institutions might benefit if nationwide branch banking is permitted. We will also be able to see how various banking institutions have laid the groundwork for nationwide banking.

The banking industry in the United States is unique in comparison to other advanced industrial countries. We do not permit nationwide branch banking in the United States, even though just about every nation in the free world offers this convenience to customers. Thus a fragmented structure has resulted that came into existence primarily from a series of state and federal laws that have limited both the product markets and geographical areas in which each banking firm may operate. Banking is the only industry to lag behind the geographical nationalization of our business and commerce. These laws are now under considerable challenge by legislative action and pressure from the industry.

Regulation is often dependent upon the nature of the economy or social concern. The increasing amount of regulation imposed upon business has resulted from heightened awareness of environmental and consumer issues. For example, increased government pressure has been placed upon banks to make mortgage money available to certain neighborhoods. This current situation differs markedly from that of the Depression era, when banking regulation was created to protect the consumer from bank failure and to shield the banks from assuming poor credit risks. Most significant banking legislation has followed major problems in the banking industry or has reflected the special needs of government. Many new government agencies have been formed in an attempt to deal with new banking problems, markets, and structure. To avoid the overlap among these regulatory agencies (see Figure 2-1), some experts have suggested that banking regulation be concentrated in one agency. However, there has been no strong unified interest on the part of financial institutions or the public to bring about integrated regulations.

It is possible that with the blurring of the functions of our depository institutions one regulatory authority will be established for these banking entities. Further, since maintaining confidence in the depository insurance system is extremely important, a merger between the *Federal Deposit Insurance Corporation (FDIC)* and the *Federal Savings and Loan Insurance Corporation (FSLIC)* might be considered a good idea. The ample resources of the former and the potential lack of resources of the latter (because of failing savings and loan associations) may bring about this merger. If this does not occur the FSLIC might have to be strengthened considerably by a government guarantee.

In many respects our financial system is flexible and efficient. Consequently, if some regulatory or legal restriction prevents a particular kind of financial institution from performing its economic function, the financial system develops another means of performing the same function. The economic incentives for circumventing these regulations and restrictions have been great, leading to many fundamental changes in the way that financial institutions conduct their business.[1]

While the *Bank Holding Company Act* forces the separation of banking from commerce, the *Savings and Loan Holding Company Act* does not. There-

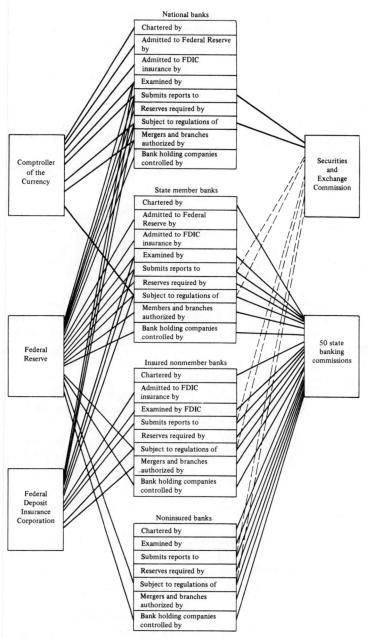

FIGURE 2-1 Regulatory powers governing national and state member banks. (*From T. G. Herrick, Bank Analysts Handbook, 1978. Reprinted by permission of John Wiley & Sons, Inc.*)

fore, commercial and industrial firms can acquire a savings and loan association, but cannot acquire a commercial bank. These industrial firms have the potential of providing nationwide banking services, given the increased powers allowed to the thrifts and the developments in the electronic transfer of funds. The entry of insurance, brokerage, and other financial firms into retail consumer banking through money market funds and the acquisition by commercial and industrial firms of thrifts means that the division of banking from commerce is now a matter of history. These are just two examples of how the financial system circumvents arbitrary regulations and laws.[2]

REGULATION AND
DEREGULATION
Let us now look at some of the key laws and regulations which impede banks. There are five major regulations which have either restricted banking activity or have placed banks at a disadvantage in competing with NDIs:

1 The McFadden Act (1927) and the Douglas Amendment to the Bank Holding Company Act (1970), which restrict interstate branching.
2 The Glass-Steagall Act (1933), which separates commercial and investment banking.
3 The Bank Holding Company Act (1960) and its amendment (1970), which limit activities to those considered "closely related" to commercial banking by the *Federal Reserve Board of Governors.*
4 Federal Reserve Regulation Q (1933), which restricts rates paid to suppliers of funds.
5 The Federal Reserve Act (1913), which established *reserve requirements* against deposits for member banks. This was later called Federal Reserve Regulation D.

Unencumbered by these regulations, some NDIs have exploited this competitive advantage by offering an array of financial products that compete with services traditionally provided by banks. While banks may not branch out across state lines, Merrill Lynch has 476 domestic offices with a representative within 25 miles of 75 percent of the population. Sears, with its 859 retail stores, has even better access to potential customers.

The process of financial innovation has been shaped not only by the differential regulatory burden but also by the technological advances and cost reductions in data processing, communications, and *electronic funds transfer systems (EFTS).* It is doubtful whether money market funds (offering checking privileges, one-day transfers, and small minimum denominations) would have grown so dramatically if the costs of processing and maintaining individual accounts and portfolios had not dropped considerably and if interest rates had not risen to such high levels. The checking account facility offering instant liquidity at money market funds also contributed to fund growth.[3]

The concern over the health of the housing industry and mortgage lenders following the disintermediation that took place at depository institutions during the credit crunches of 1966 and 1969 led to the appointment of a commission to study the problems and make recommendations. In 1971, the President's Commission on Financial Structure and Regulation (the Hunt Commission) recommended expanded powers for savings and loan associations and other mortgage lenders. The Hunt Commission recommended that thrifts be permitted to:

1 Make consumer and construction loans
2 Remove certain geographic restrictions on their lending activities
3 Extend the maturity of their liabilities
4 Remove interest rate ceilings for some deposits
5 Offer checking account services

These recommendations have been substantially incorporated into the *Depository Institutions Deregulation and Monetary Control Act of 1980* (*DIDMCA*).

This act contains a number of major provisions that should alter the nature of the banking industry. These include:

1 Subjecting any depository institution offering transaction accounts to universal reserve requirements set by the Federal Reserve
2 Opening the discount window at the Federal Reserve to all depository institutions
3 Eliminating interest rate ceilings on deposits (Regulation Q) by 1986
4 Permitting all depository financial institutions to offer NOW accounts
5 Allowing thrift institutions to lend up to 20 percent of assets in consumer loans, commercial paper, and corporate debt securities
6 Removing state usury ceiling on mortgage rates for 3 years
7 Offering Federal Reserve services to members and nonmembers on an equal basis

As part of this legislation, a committee called the Depository Institutions Deregulatory Committee (DIDC) was created to provide for the orderly implementation of certain sections of the statute. This committee was established by the DIDMCA to supervise the phase-out of deposit rate ceilings. It is chaired by the Federal Reserve Board Chairman and has, as members, the chairmen of the Federal Home Loan Bank Board, the Federal Deposit Insurance Corporation, the National Credit Union Association Board, and the secretary of the Treasury.

The DIDC had originally opted for gradual deregulation of the financial services industry for fear of imperiling the thrift industry. The committee initially refused to grant a market rate (a super NOW account) that would permit depository institutions a transaction account competitive with money market funds and also refused to raise the rates on passbook accounts. The Committee was accused of sacrificing a healthy banking industry to save a thrift industry which is no longer financially viable. It was argued that savings and loan associations are no longer considered a source of cheap mortgage money and that fast deregulation would further cripple housing. It appeared as if the DIDC was not apt to accelerate the deregulation timetable,[12] when it announced its plan to allow depository institutions the right to offer the equivalent of money market fund accounts.

Commercial banks and thrift institutions now offer two types of money market accounts. Both accounts have minimum balance requirements of $2500 and have no interest rate restrictions. If the balance dips below $2500, the rate paid would be the same 5¼ percent that applies to regular NOW accounts. One type of money market account, which has limited checking privileges of three checks per month, is open to individuals, government bodies, nonprofit organizations, and corporations. The second account, allowing unlimited check-writing privileges, is not currently for business use and is being referred to by some as a super NOW Account. Reserve requirements against this account are anticipated to be 12 percent. For individuals with $2500 in savings, the super NOW account could make obsolete the traditional checking and passbook savings accounts.

In addition, the minimum balance requirements were reduced to $2500 on all savings certificates which have maturities of 7 days to 6 months. The minimum balances had been $20,000 for accounts with maturities from 7 to 31 days and $10,000 for 13-week and 26-week deposits. The deregulation committee will probably consider speeding up the process of deregulating other bank and thrift institution interest rates. It has already removed government-imposed interest rate ceilings from deposits that mature in 3½ years or more and from deposits in IRA and Keogh retirement accounts.

If regulations had remained unchanged, relative production costs and higher money market rates to consumers would have continued to favor NDIs and would have resulted in a further decrease in the share of the financial services market held by depository institutions. However, depository institutions are expected to be more competitive with NDIs because of their insured money market accounts. Nonetheless, the cost of these funds should tighten the squeeze on the profit margins of the banks and increase the importance of their asset-liability management.

Successful innovation by unregulated NDIs increases the probability that the regulatory burden on banks will be reduced further and that banks will change the way they price services. There seems to be increasing sentiment in regulatory agencies and in Congress to ease the product, price, and geographic limitations currently imposed on banks. Banks will most likely unbundle charges for the separate services that they provide to depositors, offer loans priced in nontraditional ways (cost plus pricing), and place greater emphasis on the flow of assets through their books than on the stock of assets on them.

Some of the larger commercial banks want to be able to branch into other states and underwrite corporate and revenue bonds. Some banks would like to be able to sell life, auto, and homeowner's insurance through their branch systems or through mass marketing campaigns conducted by mail. After all, commercial banks have been permitted to sell credit insurance, while savings banks in New York, Connecticut, and Massachusetts have been permitted to sell limited amounts of life insurance. The resistance from most independent banks germane to interstate banking remains solid as does the investment banking industry's objection to the *underwriting* of both corporate and revenue bonds.

EVOLUTION One salient aspect of banking in recent years has been the great rise in the number of branches. Commercial bank branch offices, for example, expanded in the post-World War II period from fewer than 5000 in 1950 to almost 40,000 in 1980. This happened because of (1) the shift in population from heavily banked central cities to lightly banked suburbs; (2) advances in communications, data processing, and fund transfers that permitted efficient management of branch systems; (3) Regulation Q deposit ceilings that both encouraged competition through convenience banking and kept the cost of household deposits relatively low.[4]

During the period 1970–81, some important changes took place in banking. The bank holding company form of organization increased in importance, legislation established limitations on the nonbank activities of bank holding companies, and, although restrictions on *branch banking* remain, many states liberalized their branching or unit banking laws

TABLE 2-1
GROWTH OF BANK BRANCHES AND BANK HOLDING COMPANIES, 1969–1980

	BRANCHING			CONCENTRATION BANKING DEPOSITS		ASSETS HELD BY BANK HOLDING COMPANIES	
	NUMBER OF COMMERCIAL BANKS OPERATING BRANCHES		NUMBER OF BRANCHES OPERATED	10 LARGEST BANKS	100 LARGEST BANKS	SUBSIDI- ARIES OF BANK HOLDING COMPANIES	MULTI- BANK HOLDING COMPANIES
Year end 1969	3794	(27.7%)	19,985	20.2%	47.3%	38.4%	19.0%
Year end 1980	6859	(46.2%)	38,355	17.9%	45.4%	74.1%	35.7%

SOURCE: *Federal Reserve Bulletin*, April 1982.

as the movement toward more extensive branching continued. Banking data also indicate a modest trend toward more extensive branching as well as toward reduced deposit concentration in the largest commercial banks on both the national and local levels (see Table 2-1).

By mid-1982, expected changes in the financial services industry and within the financial system suggested that evolution might give way to revolution in the sense of more rapid change in the structure of our financial intermediaries. The rapid growth of EFTS, NOW accounts, and money market funds, the removal of some deposit rate ceilings, the anticipated extension of commercial banking powers to surviving thrift institutions, the likelihood of nationwide branch banking, plus the enormous growth of NDIs as providers of financial services should all act as catalysts in changing the structure of the financial services industry. While commercial banks have reached the limit of the types of acquisitions they can make without major modification of Federal Reserve policy, other firms such as insurance companies, brokerage firms, retailers, and financial service giants have been active in creating multiproduct financial intermediaries.[5]

It is interesting to note that a number of *money center* bank holding companies already possess nationwide finance companies. For example, Citicorp has a potential national distribution system of its own with 170 consumer finance offices in 27 states. These offices could be turned into deposit-taking establishments when interstate banking is permitted. The signs could be changed from Citicorp to Citibank, while teller's windows and drive-in facilities might be added to accept deposits. It will certainly be cheaper to convert finance company offices into branches which accept deposits than to buy a bank at a multiple of book value.[6]

The office of the Comptroller of the Currency approved the application of Citibank in New York to set up investment trust funds using pools of individual retirement accounts. Nonbank investment advisers offer a wide choice of ways to invest assets in IRA accounts, including conservative certificates of deposit as well as certain riskier investments. Until this ruling, *Individual Retirement Accounts (IRAs)* at banks had been largely limited to conservative savings vehicles. The permission from the Comptroller provides Citibank with yet another means to tackle nonbank financial companies head on. This ruling by the Comptroller of the Currency also further blurs the distinctions among financial institutions.

Initially, banks attempted to circumvent the regulatory restraint against offering money market funds and investment banking activities by setting up sweep arrangements for customers and by entering the retail security business by purchasing limited-purpose brokerage firms. One-stop shopping for financial services scored another advance when several large banks and insurance companies announced forays into the securities and brokerage field. Bank of America Corporation, Chase Manhattan Corporation, Citicorp, Citizens and Southern, First Pennsylvania Corporation, and Union Planters have either acquired or plan to acquire or set up discount brokerage operations.

These purchases or agreements were made because it was felt that they broadened the base of available consumer financial services. The discounters should be profitable and should offer banks potential synergies with the higher-income, upscale customer base of the brokerage firms. The banks would also be acquiring an interstate financial services network. Though banks have long been able to execute stock trades on behalf of customers, Bank of America's bid was the first time since the Great Depression that a U.S. bank holding company was permitted to buy a brokerage firm. Since Charles Schwab & Company transacts no securities underwriting or other activity from which banks are legally excluded, the *Federal Reserve* approved the acquisition. There are more changes to come. One way or another, banks will enable customers to maintain deposits, make payments, and obtain credit without the need for a bank visit. Usury laws will ultimately be changed and consumer banking should again become profitable. A caveat to this is that the eventual lifting of *Regulation Q* will increase the cost of deposits to banks. Many large banks will want to compete for consumer business. However, this competition may take a different form in the future. Nonlocal banks may seek to sign up banks rather than consumers. The local bank would be provided with a system by which it could offer services to its depositors and others in its market, while the local bank will pay processing fees to the nonlocal originator of the services. The local banks will need this capability in order to match the large regional banks and money center banks which may be competing for the local bank's customer.[7]

For example, a number of major bank holding companies might begin to franchise their name, expertise, and technology. This franchising concept would also offer a major opportunity to preserve the nation's independent banking system. Banks that become franchises might change their names to First Interstate Bank or First National City Bank of their home, city, state, or locality. They would have access to a wide range of products and services provided by First Interstate or First National City. Customers of all banks participating in the system would be able to cash checks and use the ATMs at any member bank throughout the country because all the banks would be linked through a single computer system that would make a customer's account information immediately available. System member banks would have access to expensive technology with a small initial investment.

San Francisco-based First Nationwide Savings, the sixth largest savings and loan association, with offices in California, Florida, and New York, will launch a franchise program for thrifts under which they would share costs, product development, and marketing clout. Under the franchise plan, participants will be offered shared data processing, interstate customer transactions including shared ATMs, and the commercial leasing and real estate development of First Nationwide.

Technological change is expected to continue to have an impact on banking. EFTS will not only impact the deposit, payment, and credit functions, but will also affect the geographical and numerical composition of the banking industry. Since even small businesses will be able to utilize the services of banks at considerable distances, competition in bank markets should intensify. This raises the question of the continued viability of the thousands of small banks which are now geographically protected.

We are already seeing a considerable amount of activity by out-of-state banks utilizing a variety of devices that include loan production offices, *Edge Act Corporations* (See Figure 2-2), holding company subsidiaries (particularly finance, leasing, and mortgage companies), in addition to foreign bank representative offices, agencies, and branches. While these operating units cannot do everything that a bank or bank branch can do, they can be effective competitors in many types of businesses. This activity is growing and will continue to grow without any liberalization of barriers to interstate banking.[8]

The merger movement within banking will be encouraged by the desire to diversify geographically, especially if interstate banking is

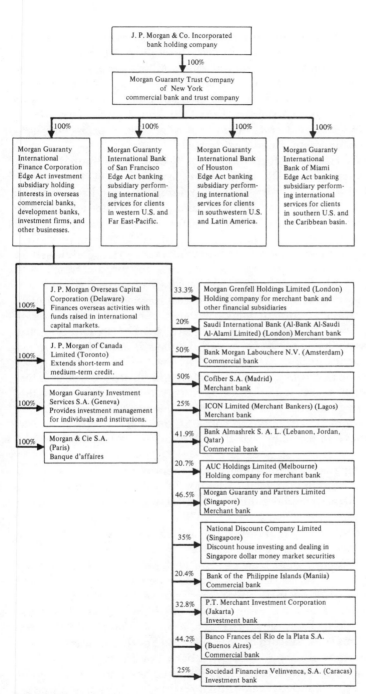

FIGURE 2-2 "Edge Act" subsidiaries of Morgan Guaranty Trust Company of New York, 1975. (*From J. P. Morgan and Company, Inc., Annual Report 1976.*)

permitted. Merger and acquisition activity in rapid growth areas would be particularly active. In a general sense, the supply of banks for acquisition will be those troubled institutions and smaller banks who are hurt by burdensome regulations, the lifting of geographical restrictions, capital shortages, and technological change. Interstate combinations such as the merging of troubled thrift institutions into a larger thrift institution in a different state may act as a catalyst in promoting geographical expansion on a nationwide basis.

Of course, a restrictive factor to interstate banking is limited capital. Some of the large banks that might be expected to be in the forefront of interstate banking activity are only minimally capitalized and will have to raise additional capital to expand. Select banks will need to borrow money if they are buying a bank stock selling at a higher price-to-earnings ratio than that of their own stock. Issuing new stock at less than book value in order to buy banks when the stock is selling at one or two times book value is not going to appear attractive to many banks. Also, foreign banks may be at an advantage when interstate banking is allowed because The Federal Reserve does not regulate the capitalization of foreign banks. Foreign banks generally operate with lower levels of capital than domestic banks.[9] In addition, the Federal Reserve has already permitted Barclays Bank, a British Bank, to open branches in both California and New York State.

One of the major difficulties in projecting the future growth of interstate banking has to do with foreseeing the future of consumer banking, a subject we will discuss in a later chapter. It is possible that consumer banking will not be attractive to some banks in the future now that banks will have to pay more for their deposits in money market fund accounts.

Another way that banks are positioning themselves for the possibility of nationwide banking is by the formation of regional banking *consortia*. Consortia of large regional banks may be established to compete with the large money center banks who will be seeking out-of-state consumer business, directly or indirectly. These consortia will also compete against the money center banks for wholesale business on both the national and international fronts. Also, with the increasing diversity and sophistication of services demanded, interstate mergers may be the only way banking institutions can achieve the corporate forms and capital base needed to compete effectively in the delivery of technologically advanced electronic services. For example, the Trust Company of Georgia, Amsouth Bancorp of Alabama, and South Carolina National Corporation, three leading southeastern bank holding companies, have indicated that they would invest $2 million in one another on a joint basis. Although the moves were initially made for defensive purposes to help avoid a takeover attempt by another corporation, the banks are also attempting to establish a working relationship where it is possible that the arrangements could form the basis for an interstate bank holding company or merger should the laws change.

There are other examples of interstate bank investments that seem to be paving the way for nationwide banking:

☐ Citicorp invested $12 million in Central National Chicago Corporation in a nonvoting preferred stock and warrant arrangement.

☐ Texas Commerce Bankshares has acquired a 4.9 percent interest in banks in Wyoming, Colorado, Louisiana, and Oklahoma, while the Provident Bank of Philadelphia held stock ownership positions in other banks throughout the country.

☐ Marine Midland Banks purchased $2.7 million of newly issued common stock of Industrial Valley Bank & Trust Company (Philadelphia area) and $77.3 million of nonvoting preferred stock with warrants. The New York bank has also made a potential $139 million investment in Centran Corporation (Cleveland) through a nonvoting preferred stock and warrants arrangement.

☐ Chase Manhattan reached an agreement in principal to make a $125 million investment and financing with Equimark Corporation and Equibank, involving nonvoting preferred debt and an option to acquire Equibank stock.

☐ First Bank Systems has announced a linkage with Banks of Iowa, and First National Boston has a similar arrangement with Casco Northern Corporation.

☐ Chemical New York Corporation has attempted to enter into a merger agreement with Florida National Banks of Florida.

☐ Girard Company in Pennsylvania (now a subsidiary of Mellon) purchased the "troubled" Farmers Bank of Delaware.

☐ NCNB has a special "grandfathered" advantage to acquire banks in Florida and has begun to do just that.

A bank's decision to expand geographically (apart from regulatory consideration germane to adequate capital and legality) is also concerned with bank management's decision as to whether it wishes to be acquired, expand, or attempt to keep the status quo. A bank can expand via branches, automated teller machines, or nonbank subsidiaries. The individual regional bank will have to decide whether it wishes to expand outright, build correspondent banking networks, become part of a national consortium of regional banks, or become the local (independently owned) franchise of one of the larger money center banks. Some banks will choose to purchase services from larger banks and still remain independent, while some banks will choose to be acquired. Some institutions will seek to remain independent by offering highly personalized services and certain specialties that are unique or highly desirable to a segment of the marketplace.

Some acquisition-minded banks may be interested in acquiring a mutual savings bank or savings and loan association. There is no logical reason to prohibit bank holding companies from acquiring thrift institutions. Indeed, the Justice Department has authorized the Federal Reserve to approve such acquisitions. The reluctance of the regulatory authorities to approve the savings and loan business as an allowable activity for bank holding companies has simply been a matter of potential political repercussion. The key aspect of banks buying thrift institutions is that it permits the bank to expand on an interstate basis. Justice Department approval might help solve the thrift problems because expansion-minded commercial banks might be willing to pay substantial premiums to acquire the right to operate consumer banking activities on an interstate basis.[10] As a matter of fact, Chase Manhattan and Citicorp have already expressed an interest in acquiring a thrift institution. Citicorp has apparently won its bid to acquire the troubled Fidelity Savings Association of San Francisco.

The money market fund accounts available at banks and thrift institutions will enable traditional depository institutions to recapture some of the funds that they lost to NDIs because of noncompetitive short-term interest rates. However, these new higher-yielding accounts will most likely hurt earnings of some institutions in the short run as consumers draw money out of the currently regulated accounts that provide depository institutions with inexpensive sources of money. For example, deposits at the end of August 1982 at commercial banks totaled $231 billion in non-interest-paying checking accounts, $90 billion in interest-paying checking accounts, and $342 billion in regular passbook savings accounts. Much of that money could be transferred to new higher-paying money market fund accounts.

Although the banking lobby won the right to offer money market funds, it did not gain the right to underwrite or sell property and casualty insurance during the 1982 congressional session.

After a major lobbying campaign, insurers won provisions in banking legislation passed by Congress that significantly limit the ability of bank holding companies to underwrite or sell property and casualty insurance. The bill prohibits bank holding companies with assets of more than $50 million from selling or underwriting most forms of insurance other than credit life, credit disability, and unemployment insurance. Any holding company insurance activity previously authorized by the Federal Reserve Board can continue. About a thousand companies will be covered by the grandfather clause. Also, there are no restrictions on the insurance activities of holding companies in towns with populations of 5000 or less or on the sale of property insurance or loan collateral held by finance company subsidiaries of bank holding companies.

Although banking deregulation germane to interest rate ceilings, interstate banking, and the gradual blurring of the distinctions among financial service industry participants should occur, it is likely that legislative deregulation of the barriers separating the banking and securities industries may take some time in coming. Many analysts believe that legislation tends to follow the events of the marketplace and that congressional action on complete financial deregulation will not occur until it has in fact already become a reality. While a salient obstacle to complete financial deregulation is the conflicting vested interest of the different financial intermediaries, there are other key political issues whose consideration may substantially delay legislative action such as:[11]

☐ The issue of consolidation that would occur in the aftermath of the elimination of both the McFadden and the Glass-Steagall Acts. The resulting consolidation could lead to a situation where only a few corporations controlled most of our country's financial services.
☐ The channeling of deposit flows from economically stagnant or declining areas of the country into loans in growing regions where opportunities for profit might be greater and credit risks lower.
☐ The potential shifting of control of the nation's capital raising function away from independent investment bankers into the hands of multi-industry corporations who might have specific vested interests.

NOTES

1 J. L. Pierce, "Financial Institutions in a Revolutionary Era," Testimony before the Committee on Banking, Finance, and Urban Affairs, U.S. House of Representatives, December 10, 1981, p. 2.

2 Ibid., pp. 6–7.

3 "Shaping the Financial Revolution," *The Chase Economic Observer*, vol. I, no. 4, July–August 1981, pp. 3–4.

4 G. G. Kaufmann, "The Changing Competitive Environment," *Proceedings on the Future of the Financial Services Industry*, Federal Reserve Bank of Atlanta, 1981, p. 92.

5 A. A. Heggestad, "Structural Implications of Consolidation in Banking," *Proceedings*

on the Future of the Financial Services Industry, Federal Reserve Bank of Atlanta, 1981, pp. 85–88.

6 *Fortune,* December 28, 1981.

7 P. M. Horvitz, "Geographical Restrictions on Financial Institutions," *Proceedings on the Future of the Financial Services Industry,* Federal Reserve Bank of Atlanta, 1981, p. 44.

8 Ibid., p. 45.

9 Ibid., p. 41.

10 Ibid., p. 43.

11 J. Rosenthal, "Financial Deregulation and the Securities Industry," *Appreciation Potentials,* Jessup and Lambert Securities Company, March 4, 1982, p. 4.

12 J. R. Burke and J. B. Moore, *Structural Changes in the Financial Services Industry,* The Robinson-Humphrey Company, Inc., May 3, 1982, p. 1.

CHAPTER
THREE

THE FINANCIAL CONGLOM- ERATES

One of the recent trends taking place in the financial services industry is the formation of financial conglomerates that are preparing to offer the American public the opportunity to buy. a wide range of financial services from single sprawling entities. Few analysts have stopped to ask whether synergy on such a large scale can really work in the financial services business. Can the diverse parts of these financial service conglomerates mesh and complement each other, leading to increased sales and reduced costs related to consolidation?

Some evidence suggests that it will be difficult to achieve these synergies, at least in the short run. Previous attempts to create synergy in the financial services industry have been somewhat disappointing. For the most part, life insurance sales by stock brokerage firms and mutual savings banks have not been a roaring success. Continental Insurance made little progress toward the synergy that was supposed to accrue from its Diners Club credit card operation or its consumer finance subsidiary (both units have been sold), while INA was never able to sell insurance through its Blyth Eastman Dillon subsidiary. In addition, CNA Insurance had great difficulty entering the mutual fund business in the late 1960s, while Prudential has not been able to profitably diversify into the property and casualty insurance field. American Express was never able to parlay its 25 percent holding in Donaldson, Lufkin, and Jenrette between 1971 and 1975 into any great advantage.

Of course, significant cross-selling opportunities can accrue to financial conglomerates as well as increased opportunities for mass marketing of additional services. There are also opportunities to eventually consolidate operations and utilize available computer capacity. However, it may take years to effectively achieve these synergies. You cannot simply press a button and make it happen; many details must be worked out. Some mergers will be successful; others will end up in divestiture. Nevertheless, the trend toward financial conglomeration is real and likely to continue in the future as witnessed by the large number of nonbank companies that have become significant factors in the financial services business:

ITT (Hartford Fire, ITT Credit, ITT Financial)

General Electric (General Electric Credit)

RCA (CIT)

Sears (Dean Witter, Coldwell Banker, Allstate Savings and Loan Association, Allstate Insurance, credit cards)

Beneficial (Beneficial Finance, Beneficial Savings Bank, Beneficial National Bank)

Greyhound (Greyhound leasing, money orders, insurance services)

Transamerica (Transamerica Insurance)

Prudential (Bache, PruLease, life insurance, property and casualty insurance, annuities, pension management)

National Steel (First Nationwide Savings, the largest federally chartered multistate savings and loan association)

American Express (Shearson/American Express, Fireman's Fund, international banking, credit cards, travelers' checks and services)

Baldwin United (MGIC Investment Corporation)

Gulf and Western (Associates Corporation)

Merrill Lynch (insurance, real estate, financial advising, brokerage, relocation management, mortgage bankers)

Control Data (Commercial Credit Corporation)

In all probability, the financial services industry will be considerably less fragmented in the future. It might be comprised of giant-sized institutions, the largest of which will offer a complete spectrum of banking, insurance, and other financial services. In fact, as financial institutions grow in both size and scope of function over the next 20 years, it may be difficult to distinguish between Sears, Citicorp, American Express, and Merrill Lynch from the standpoint of financial services offered.[1] Financial institutions, especially banks, will diversify even further as the giants offer more homogeneous, depersonalized products and seek greater market shares. As long as service is acceptable, these institutions should be able to provide customers with basic products at a lower cost by avoiding duplication of effort and by utilizing new technology. However, there will still be room for institutions that will be able to carve out a niche in the financial marketplace by offering exceptional personal or specialized services. Financial speciality stores or boutiques may even develop as many individuals prefer special attention and a choice of products and services.

The future of the financial services industry will also be greatly influenced by government regulatory process in the following ways:

1 In the banking and insurance sectors, some hardships of regulation appear to be lessening. The distinction on the retail banking front among depository institutions has faded. Interest rate ceilings on the various forms of bank deposits will probably be relaxed sooner than the suggested deregulation in 1986; geographical limitations to branch banking within the United States should diminish.

2 The political process is currently placing pressure on the insurance industry at the state levels. It appears as if there is an attempt to use the insurance mechanism in dealing with perceived problems of social inequalities and as an instrument of social reform. Some states are applying political pressure to hold down personal automobile insurance costs and to change the techniques used by insurance companies to price their product.

3 The rapid development of technology is making obsolete the geographic restrictions of the McFadden Act. Electronic funds transfer systems (EFTS) and the widespread use of national credit cards have facilitated the ability of banks to conduct business beyond state boundaries. The holding company umbrella has also enabled these institutions to offer a broad spectrum of financial services nationwide. Bank holding companies have stretched existing loopholes to the limit, pushing far beyond the original intentions of regulators and lawmakers.

4 With the relaxation of regulation, branch banks could offer life, health, homeowners', and auto insurance by the year 2000. Today's insurance company may still be the underwriter, but the banking system may become the distributor, thereby replacing the indepen-

dent agent over the next two decades. Insurance could be sold at the local branch or through bank mailings with a credit card. Such blurring of the distinctions among the functions of most American financial intermediaries will probably take place over the next two decades. The continental Europeans have already taken advantage of a legal system which permits such *universal banking,* i.e., the selling of all financial services through a single intermediary.

5 Although the Glass-Steagall Act of 1933 purports to separate the U.S. securities industry from banking, recent events indicate that universal banking may not be as far away or as difficult to accomplish as originally imagined:

☐ Banks sell securities. Citibank has formed a securities company for bank customers behind the protective curtain of its trust department and has purchased a discount broker; Bank of America and Union Planters have also purchased discount brokers.
☐ Insurance companies actively pursue short-term commercial and industrial loans as well as longer-term private placements and mutual fund business. They have also acquired brokerage firms.
☐ Many brokerage firms and some mutual savings banks sell insurance.
☐ A number of brokerage firms and financial holding companies operate international banks.

6 The retail banking markets were dominated by thrift institutions, credit unions, commercial banks, and consumer finance companies until money market mutual funds became popular, and "near-banks" such as Sears, American Express, and Merrill Lynch began to display their muscle in the consumer financial marketplace.

The potential impact of these near-banks on the financial markets is enormous. Banks and savings and loan associations are bogged down in a quagmire of Depression-era regulations that prevent them from branching across state lines, shut the door on domestic investment banking, and sharply limit subsidiary activity. Near-banks, on the other hand, are scarcely touched by such rules because they do not accept deposits. They are less restricted as to the business functions they can perform and the business locations they can choose.

Let us now look at some of these financial conglomerates and see their strengths, weaknesses, and likely evolution.

MERRILL LYNCH Although Merrill Lynch is best known as a retail stock brokerage firm, it performs a complete array of investment banking services. In addition, the company offers rather extensive institutional and economics research to support its wholesale effort to buy and sell stocks and bonds. Its Capital Markets Group is actively engaged in merchant banking, institutional sales, trading, *arbitrage, block positioning,* and *underwriting.*

The greatest growth at Merrill Lynch has come in its retail or consumer activities. Its money market funds and Cash Management Account (CMA) have attracted a plethora of new customers that offer the potential to become retail brokerage customers. The CMA combines a securities account, a money market fund, a VISA debit card, and access to liquidity through a credit card or checking account arrangements via Banc One of Columbus, Ohio. The company also offers credit cards to its retail customers.

Merrill Lynch has also begun to sell insurance through its brokers in close to 500 domestic offices. There appears to be great potential in consumer insurance sales that can be made through stockbrokers once the brokers are taught how to sell insurance and to better understand the products they sell and the needs of consumers.

The company has become active in selling *tax shelters* in the form of real estate, motion picture investments, as well as oil and gas drilling limited partnerships. It also offers commodity services as well as investment and economic services to both individuals and institutions. The company has also begun selling CDs for Banc One of Columbus and Home Federal Savings and Loan of San Diego from whom they receive a commission. As custodian of the account, Merrill Lynch has created a secondary market for these consumer-oriented 3½- to 5-year CDs, allowing consumers who wish to sell, a quick, no-penalty exit. In addition to providing a new source of fee income, the sale of CDs is a hedge against a likely loss of customers from its $30 billion family of money market funds should their appeal diminish under a falling interest rate scenario.

The company also has an active real estate subsidiary that offers to buy and sell homes and commercial properties. It offers relocation services as well as rental services. The company has also entered the domestic consumer credit market by offering a revolving credit account secured by a borrower of home equity. The company will offer a line of credit equal to as much as 70 percent of the appraised value of the borrower's home, minus any mortgage outstanding. Merrill Lynch will issue the borrower a special Visa card and a checkbook. The borrower will have a defined line of credit at a cost that will float at 3.5 percentage points above the prime rate with a floor of 14 percent. In addition the customer will have to pay a $200 fee for a special home appraisal and paperwork, a $35 annual fee, and a fee of 1.5 percent

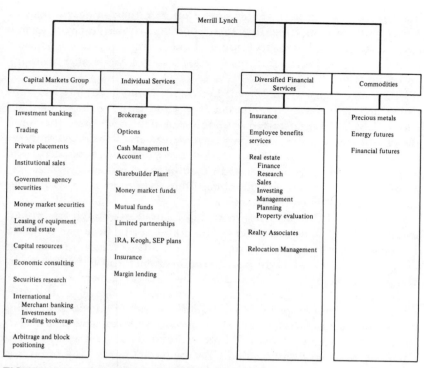

FIGURE 3-1   Organization chart for Merrill Lynch.

of the credit line. All these services appear to be part of a corporate plan for Merrill to become a complete financial supermarket for investors (see Figure 3-1).

THE NEW SEARS   Sears Roebuck, in one sense, is even more of a financial supermarket than Merrill Lynch. Through Allstate, its property, casualty, and life insurance subsidiary; Dean Witter; Coldwell Banker; its ownership of the eleventh largest savings and loan association in California with $3 billion in assets and a small commercial bank in Chicago; its nearly 4000 outlets in department stores and catalog offices; a new check-processing service to be offered in conjunction with credit unions; and its base of 25 million active credit card holders, Sears may well be a model of future banking concerns (see Figure 3-2).

The Chicago-based Sears has a huge in-house data base on consumer credit which will become the nucleus for the carefully targeted selling of loans, money market funds, stocks, and other instruments. A recent Roper organization poll found Sears to be "viewed most favorably" by consumers who rated it against other corporations. This acceptance should offer Sears an edge over competitive financial institutions. Sears seems ready to launch an array of additional services that will include:

☐ The formation of a world trading company.
☐ The provision of retirement account opportunities for its customers.
☐ A *debit card* that could be used to endow the new money market fund accounts with savings and checking account privileges.
☐ A universal financial card capable of handling practically all household financial transactions.
☐ A move into secured and unsecured personal lending, including homeowners' loans that should rival finance companies, banks, and thrifts.
☐ A pioneering system in two-way communications with the home through computers and telephone for financial and consumer product transactions.
☐ A national hookup of *automated teller machines* (*ATMs*) in Sears retail stores which could hook up to banklike Sears merchandise credit accounts, allowing customers to draw cash, take small personal loans through prearranged lines of credit, deposit money, or make merchandise, mortgage, insurance premium, or stock purchase payments. Through agreements that Sears could make with certain banks, cus-

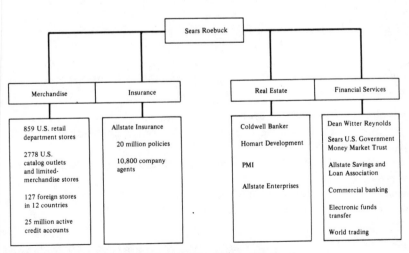

FIGURE 3-2 Organization chart for Sears Roebuck.

tomers of those banks could use ATMs at Sears stores to tap their savings or checking accounts or even to pay bills.

A Standard Research Institute study shows the vast potential and scope of Sears' retail accounts:

☐ While 25 million households actively use Sears cards, 48 million or 57 percent of all households hold one. This compares with 53 percent for Visa, 39 percent for J. C. Penney, 27 percent for Montgomery Ward, and 11 percent for American Express;
☐ Among households with more than $36,000 annual income, 70 percent had Sears cards, while among households with net worth in excess of $500,000, 76 percent had Sears cards;
☐ Fewer than 9 percent of Sears active credit card holders have brokerage accounts, while they hold close to two-thirds of the passbook savings dollars in the country.

This information suggests that Dean Witter could gain millions of new, well-heeled customers, and Sears customers would eventually be able to buy a house, obtain a mortgage, furnish the house, insure it and their own lives, invest idle funds in a high-yield, low-risk money market fund, and buy securities—all from the ultimate in one-stop shopping. However, retailing and financial services may be difficult to combine since the businesses have different rhythms, cash needs, and selling methods.[2]

Edward Teller, Sears chairman, told a meeting of the Economics Club of Chicago that Sears' goal is "to provide more goods and services to more people in the future." Sears plans to expand in the financial services area by providing a full range of financial services, including electronic funds transfer throughout the United States.

Sears has opened up experimental financial service centers in eight stores in major metropolitan areas. The financial centers are staffed by about a half dozen people that represent:

1 Allstate for auto, home, and life insurance
2 Dean Witter for investing in bonds, stocks, IRAs, and money market instruments
3 Coldwell Banker for buying or selling a house, a business property, or land
4 Allstate Savings and Loan in the California stores for branch banking, mortgage loans, and insured money market accounts.

These financial service centers are located in high traffic areas of the stores where Sears hopes to lure shoppers to sell them insurance, IRAs, stocks, bonds, and land. The centers contain hands-on computers designed to entice customers to have fun and relax so that a representative can explain the array of financial services that Sears has available. Sears strategy is based on generating the same lifelong customer loyalty for its financial services that they have earned for their tools and appliances. The success of Sears' strategy is dependent upon whether its traditional customers need and will actually use the Sears financial centers.

The effect of Sears new acquisitions on revenues, assets, and profits is shown in the following tables. Most data is for the year ended December 31, 1981; Dean Witter data is for the year ended August 31, 1981.

In revenues, merchandising still exceeds financial services:

	Revenues, in Billions of Dollars
Sears merchandising	18.2
Sears financial services	9.2
Allstate group	6.8
Credit operations	1.0
Dean Witter	0.9
Coldwell Banker group	0.5

Financial services, however, now exceed merchandising in assets and in profits:

	Assets, in Billions of Dollars	Profits, in Millions of Dollars
Sears merchandising	6.5	352
Sears financial services	27.3	436
Allstate group	11.5	406
Credit operations	7.3	(83)
Dean Witter	4.1	51
Coldwell Banker group	4.4	62

Moreover, Sears financial services profits are almost as large as some of the other financial giants:

	Net Income, in Millions of Dollars
Merrill Lynch	203
BankAmerica Corp.	445
Aetna Life & Casualty	462
American Express	518
Citicorp	531
Sears financial services	352

Sears credit card customers may be getting Dean Witter promotional pieces in their monthly statements. The problem is that *cross-selling* seldom seems to work as well as it might theoretically. Although mail-order marketing has worked for money market funds and some forms of life and health insurance, it does not necessarily do so for other financial products. Sears has not been particularly successful at selling Allstate auto insurance through Sears catalogs; similarly American Express has had only minimal success in selling Fireman's Fund insurance through mailings to American Express cardholders. Sales personnel are themselves a cross-selling uncertainty as only some securities brokers have been successful at selling insurance or tax shelters; sales personnel may not be willing to share their customers. Merrill Lynch, for example, has tried without much success to generate cooperation between its securities brokers and real estate brokers.

Sears recently sold its own commercial paper directly to the public, bypassing the services of investment bankers. Using its credit card customers as a marketing base, future investors should be able to purchase the notes by calling a toll-free number. This will not only place Sears in competition with commercial banks for consumer funds, but it is another reminder of banking's slackening hold on the consumer deposit market. If Sears is successful in this venture, other companies may satisfy their external financing needs in a similar manner. These companies could obtain funds at a cost under market rates, but would offer potential investors an interest rate that would be significantly above the passbook rate at banks. Avoiding the commercial banks for meeting external financing needs would be another potential blow to bank profitability.

The company's 859 stores could double as full-scale financial service branches. Interactive television could be the salient vehicle that integrates Sears' entire retail distribution system: stores, catalogs, and insurance and brokerages offices. Although the potential for cross-selling and the introduction of these new products seem quite promising, there are some potential pitfalls. As the company pushes more direct selling of merchandise and services, notably through interactive television and home computer systems, it may steal sales from its own stores.

Sears might eventually be able to close some unprofitable or superfluous stores, lease out some additional unneeded space, or cut back on personnel in stores. Equally alarming, direct selling via television or through the mail may bypass its large commissioned network at Dean Witter and Allstate. Another potential problem is that by becoming a competitor, Sears may lose current business with other financial institutions, such as the property insurance referrals Allstate gets from real estate brokers. Real estate brokers may not wish to send referrals to the local Allstate agent if they feel that they are helping a competitor in the sense that Coldwell Banker is in the real estate business.

Although the cross-selling synergies are expected to be evolutionary, there has been at least one positive accomplishment. Dean Witter Reynolds, rather than Goldman-Sachs, led a $400 million zero-coupon Eurobond issue for Sears early in 1982. However, the true test of synergism will come over the next few years when we shall see whether the diverse parts of these financial service conglomerates can mesh and act as a stimulus to each other.

AMERICAN EXPRESS The next financial services giant, American Express Company, faces a huge challenge in successfully integrating the securities firm of Shearson Loeb Rhoades, Inc. (acquired in a $1 billion stock swap) into its financial empire. This financial conglomerate with a holding company at the top is best known for its travel service and credit card business. Among its major assets are a giant-sized international bank, Warner Amex Cable Communications, Fireman's Fund insurance, and Mitchell Beazly Ltd., (a publishing company). It has also purchased a 10 percent interest in McLeon Young Weir Ltd., a major Canadian securities firm. Shearson has also purchased Foster & Marshall, one of the largest regional brokerage firms in the Northwest and Robinson-Humphrey, a major regional brokerage house in Atlanta (see Figure 3-3).

American Express is moving beyond travel and leisure dollars to vie for a central role in the money that Americans save and invest. The company is counting on two salient aspects of its business: its reach into the affluent sector of the economy through its 13 million cardholders whom it views as nearly recession-proof and through its data processing ability and information systems. Hardwich Simmons, senior executive vice president at Shearson, says, "We have a chance to build a whole new industry." American Express hopes to play a key role in the money people spend, save, and invest. The company wishes to become an omnipresent intermediary for affluent Americans, tapping into the estimated $8 trillion of personal assets in the United States.

In addition to its credit card base of customers, American Express can also reach affluent Americans through more than 4000 brokers in its Shearson system. According to Sanford I. Weil, the Shearson chairman, these sources provide "the ultimate link with the high-net-worth individual." A number of analysts believe that American Express' data processing and communications expertise gives them a leg up on Wall

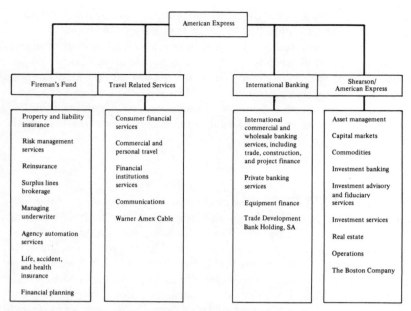

FIGURE 3-3 Organization chart for American Express.

Street rivals. The company has always considered "the effective delivery of information" a central aspect of every business that the company has entered, according to James D. Robinson III, American Express Company's chairman.

Warner Amex Cable constructs and operates cable systems that provide video programming and other services to residential and commercial subscribers often via satellite networks. Experiments on providing subscribers with a wealth of information from data banks, such as the New York Times, The Washington Post, and the Associated Press are being conducted in a joint effort between Warner Amex, Atari, and Compuserve, Inc.

Competition for "upscale" consumers of financial services is intense because most companies are targeting the same market. Many observers feel that American Express is better tapped into the "cult of affluence" than is the competition. One of the reasons for this is the belief that American Express card holders (on an average) have 2.5 times the net worth of those without a card.

Shearson, its brokerage acquisition, has not been inactive. Shearson has acquired Balcor Company, a major real estate syndicator. In addition to packaging real estate investments for investors doing business with Shearson, Balcor will develop products for overseas clients of American

Express International Banking Corporation and for customers of Fireman's Fund Insurance. The real estate acquisition also adds another facet to the fast-growing financial services empire of American Express.

At least one tangible benefit has developed from the Shearson and American Express merger. Shearson comanaged a $100 million note issue for American Express Credit Corporation, saving a fee that probably would have gone to their traditional investment banker, Paine Webber Blyth Eastman Dillon.

The company is presently gearing up for the first offspring of the Shearson and American Express marriage, a computerized cash management service called the Financial Management Account (FMA) which permits credit card and checking withdrawals from an investment account. The FMA is similar to the CMA established by Merrill Lynch. There is one modest difference, FMA customers will use an American Express Gold Card in conjunction with their account when they make a purchase. American Express will receive a discount from the merchant since its card is used. In the CMA, the customer uses a Visa card so that Merrill Lynch receives nothing from transactions.

Another kicker is the potential tie-in with Warner Amex Cable Communications which would put American Express in the forefront of electronic consumer financial transactions on their television screens. The company is exploring other sophisticated interactive home services such as electronic banking and shopping and commercial services for business. Insurance contracts and travel arrangements should eventually be available from either the home computer or cable television screens. It should also be possible to have either an airline ticket or an insurance policy printed instantly and made immediately available. The cable TV system may also have a slot where you can insert your American Express card for payment.

This cable system, with franchises in Dallas, Houston, Pittsburgh, Cincinnati, Columbus, suburban Chicago, St. Louis, and sections of New York City, will give American Express a foot in the doors of many homes and companies when all the systems are fully operational.

PRUDENTIAL-BACHE Another huge conglomerate, Prudential, the insurance giant with some 20 million life insurance policies outstanding, purchased Bache Halsey Stuart and several other regional brokerage firms in a move viewed as an attempt to gain access to higher-income clientele of the brokerage firms. The average value of a Prudential policy is only $25,000, well below the average industrial insurance policy level. Both Prudential and Bache have improved cross-

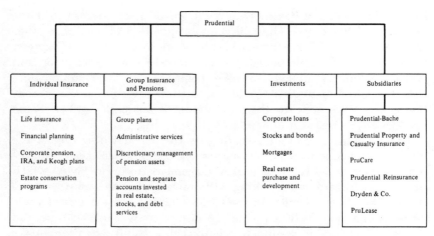

FIGURE 3-4   Organization chart for Prudential.

selling opportunities in which to offer their financial products and services. It is also further evidence of the move toward the financial variety store (see Figure 3-4).

George L. Ball, the new chief executive officer of Prudential-Bache Securities, has stated that he plans to hire well-known securities analysts in the hope that a prestigious Prudential-Bache research group will become the firm's big lure in attracting more commission income by supplying investment recommendations to institutional and individual investors. He has also publicly stated that he would like to have Prudential-Bache buy or create its own savings and loan institution.

Bache Halsey Stuart Shields, Inc. has tapped the strengths of its parent company, Prudential Insurance Company of America, to enhance a cash management service that began in the Spring of 1982. Like Merrill Lynch's highly successful Cash Management Account, the Bache Command Account will combine the high-interest income of a money market fund with the convenience of check writing and credit card withdrawals. Users of the Bache Service will:

☐ Have automatic insurance coverage to a maximum of $10 million, well in excess of the $500,000 protection provided by the Securities Investor Protection Corporation.

☐ Have access to Citicorp's Pass Word Service traveler's checks, which can be ordered by telephone and delivered.

☐ Have access to Comp-V-Card of America, Inc., a national computerized shopping service. Purchases made on a Visa card would be debited against the Bache account.

- Be able to obtain year-end statements that would tally any checks written for tax-deductible items.
- Have a sweep arrangement whereby idle cash in a Bache account would be automatically placed into a money market fund, a tax exempt securities fund, or a government securities fund, depending upon the customer's choice.
- Have to pay a $50 annual service fee and maintain a minimum balance of $20,000 to open a new account.

If Prudential can sell group life and health insurance to corporations, it may be able to sell mutual funds to workers in the form of corporate savings and investment plans through payroll deductions. People seem to feel comfortable with payroll deductions because they feel that their employer is watching over the process.

Joint marketing has already taken place with the Bache salespeople selling the Prudential-managed Chanceller Tax Manager Utility Fund. Prudential will have its sales force market certain mutual funds that are managed by Bache. Prudential expects to develop tax shelter products that will be "retailed" by Bache salespeople. The Bache corporate finance teams hope to approach some of Prudential's many midsized regional borrowers to line up possible equity underwritings. Also, Bache has acquired Elkins & Co., a Philadelphia brokerage firm, Bruns, Nordeman, Rea & Co., a New York brokerage firm, and Bateman Eichler, Hill Richards, Inc., a Los Angeles–based firm. This acquisition trend is likely to continue since Bache wanted better balance and recognized the various cost savings associated with the eventual consolidation of firms as well as the potential for increased sales and market penetration. Such mergers have become increasingly attractive because many regional companies cater heavily to the individual investor rather than to the institutional investor. The diversification by institutional brokerage and insurance companies into the regional brokerage field suggests that recognition of cross-selling opportunities and greater market penetration, more selective participation in the market for consumer financial services, as well as a movement toward the financial supermarket.

Financial conglomerates are not limited strictly to financial institutions. As a case in point, consider that commercial banking's share of the assets owned by financial institutions in the United States has dwindled from more than 57 percent in 1946 to less than 37 percent today. Of course part of this is attributable to changes in market share within the traditional financial services industry, but equally significant are the activities of enterprises operating in the financial marketplace from bases entirely outside the financial industry.

Companies whose primary business historically lies outside the financial marketplace such as GMAC, General Electric Credit, and J. C. Penney are able to generate assets and organizations in relatively unregulated environments. These assets and organizational abilities can then be brought into the financial marketplace, where they are used with growing success to compete against institutions like commercial banks. On the other hand, commercial banks are often legally barred from engaging in any other non-bank-related activity.

In early 1978, for example, the two largest chains of retail stores in the United States had installment receivables equal to more than $\frac{1}{12}$ of the total consumer installment credit in the country. Several such companies have established strong positions in the insurance industry. Altogether, the finance-related profits accruing to these "nonfinancial" companies are large. None of America's commercial banks, for example, were able to equal the 1978 financial earnings of the largest chain of retail stores, while only three equalled or surpassed those of General Motors Acceptance Corporation.

J. C. Penney Co. is another retailer entering the war of the financial service centers through an agreement with First Nationwide Savings. As a result of recent acquisitions this savings and loan association has 150 branches in California, New York, and Florida. First Nationwide intends to set up financial service centers in five Penney stores in northern California on a test basis. If the program is successful, more centers would probably follow. Penney's actions follow in the footsteps of Sears. The Kroger Co., which owns foodstores, bakeries, dairies, and drugstores, has also reached an agreement with Capital Holding Co. to undertake a similar venture.

The Penney centers will be 1500-square-foot "environments" that will combine the sale of First Nationwide deposit accounts and loans with the activities of Penney's insurance companies. J. C. Penney already has 107 insurance sales centers in its 1700 stores. Those centers sell life, health, automobile, and homeowners' insurance through the centers and directly to credit cardholders. Penney has 25 million cardholders, 16 million of whom are active users of the Penney card. First Nationwide's money market account and other financial products will be sold through the mail to Penney cardholders. First Nationwide may also sell tax preparation services at these financial service centers, individual retirement accounts, mortgages, and other loans.

CAN FINANCIAL CONGLOMERATES SUCCEED?
The actions of Sears, Merrill Lynch, and American Express suggest what might lie ahead for the financial services industry.

With a loosening of regulation, financial conglomerates that offer all financial services nationwide could emerge. The current regulations separating insurance companies, banks, and consumer finance and investment brokerages are fading, laying the foundation for the future. The real questions that must be answered are whether American consumers will really be attracted by one-stop shopping for all their financial needs and whether the environment is truly different today so that hybrid financial products and cross-selling across subsidiaries can really work in the 1980s. Recently, the advertising of financial services seems to encourage consumers to be selective, to pick and choose the best investment or vendor of services to fit a particular need. On the other hand, Wall Street firms have moved toward profitability, and public attitude is more positive toward savings and investment. A lot of careful planning will be necessary in order for the sum of the parts to add to more than the sum of separate entities.

NOTES

1 A. Gart, "The Future of the Financial Services Industry," National Association of Business Economists, Jacksonville, Florida, October 19, 1979.

2 *Business Week,* November 16, 1981.

CHAPTER
FOUR

RETAIL COMMERCIAL BANKING

Commercial banks, as we know them today, probably originated in Europe as metalsmiths expanded their trade to include money lending. The metalsmiths discovered that part of the money left with them was never withdrawn and soon began to lend it to others who would pay them interest. The first American bank to begin operation was the Bank of North America in Philadelphia in 1784.

During the eighteenth century and the first half of the nineteenth century, the key nonbank outlets that extended credit were small merchants, physicians, and pawnbrokers. The Industrial Revolution brought about changes in credit demands and institutions by making more goods available to consumers and creating a class of wage earners. The credit needs of these workers differed from the credit needs of farmers who paid off their debts when their crops were sold. In contrast, industrial wage earners received regular income and could pay back their debts on a regular basis. Accordingly, the concept of installment credit evolved, since many workers were paid low wages and required credit to raise their standard of living. These credit needs were partially satisfied by a new type of lending institution—small loan companies that concentrated on making personal loans secured by personal property or household items, with wage assignments on unsecured promissory notes. Those who could not obtain credit from legitimate small loan companies borrowed from loan sharks, who charged excessive rates of interest.

By the beginning of the twentieth century, installment credit was available throughout the United States. A direct result of the effort to curb and regulate the widespread growth of loan sharks was the development of consumer finance companies. After World War I, new types of credit institutions developed in response to the increased demand for cars and consumer appliances. Sales *finance companies,* which buy consumer installment contracts from retail dealers and provide wholesale financing for those dealers, grew from this demand. Commercial banks were the next institution to enter the consumer loan field when the National City Bank of New York opened the first personal loan department in 1928. This was followed in 1938 when John Wanamaker, a large Philadelphia department store, introduced the *revolving retail credit agreement.* The next major innovation in consumer credit was the development of the *bank credit card* in 1951 by the Franklin National Bank in New York. This plastic card was the forerunner of Visa, Master-Card, and a plethora of other credit cards issued by retail stores, oil companies, and banks. At present, commercial banks hold more *consumer credit* than any other type of financial intermediary, holding about half of the consumer credit outstanding.[1]

The market for consumer as opposed to corporate financial services is commonly called retail banking. Although both thrift institutions and commercial banks always fought for consumer deposits, they have recently been joined by the NDIs in an attempt to solicit consumer savings for their money market funds. The banks and savings and loan associations had been at a competitive disadvantage in attempting to attract deposits from individuals because they did not have an instrument that could compete effectively with the high current yield and the liquidity of money market funds. Many commercial banks have not found retail banking to be especially profitable, and most thrift institutions are currently losing money. The high costs of maintaining a branch system, the increased costs of deposits, the costs of ATMs and credit or debit cards, as well as the backup computers, software, telecommunications, check-processing expenses, and increased loan losses have caused a strain even on the banks that are thought to be well-capitalized.

Citicorp has to date been unsuccessful in making retail banking profitable despite the fact that it has invested $500 million in technology. Retail banking profitability has been handicapped by state usury law ceilings on consumer and mortgage loans as well as by the increased costs of obtaining consumer deposits. Essentially, there has been a narrowing of the spread between the cost of consumer deposits and the yield available on consumer loans. The costs involved in delivering services to individuals have also increased.

Many large commercial banks have begun to deemphasize retail banking because of these problems. In partially withdrawing from the consumer market, some banks have simply found it less costly and more convenient to buy large deposits in the money markets instead of buying small amounts from several thousand consumers. However, this is risky during periods of tight money without a large customer base of corporate and wealthy individuals that maintain certificates of deposit on a regular basis. It is important that bank officers establish a good relationship with their large depositors to ensure continuity of deposits.

Citicorp's view is that banks will need to have the best capabilities possible to process information in a profitable fashion and that electronics will ultimately dominate all aspects of the financial services business. Electronic banking and information systems will offer the customer the best possible service and information, reduce the cost of transactions for the bank, and help the bank develop fee revenues. If development of technologically based financial service product delivery systems by the large banks persists commensurate with the relaxation in geographical restrictions, considerable competitive pressure would be brought to bear on small- and medium-sized banks and thrift institutions.[2]

While mortgage loans are a major consumer business, the savings and loan associations have been the major factor in that market, with the banks only involved to a limited extent. The large commercial banks have concentrated on providing commercial and industrial loans to businesses and to a much lesser extent loans to consumers. The smaller banks have dealt largely with consumer and mortgage lending as well as loans to small companies. Finance companies, credit card companies, and retail chain stores have been among the salient competitors of commercial banks in offering consumer loans.

One way of looking at retail banking is to think of it as subdivided into two markets: a market consisting of wealthy individuals and a middle income market. The high-asset-value market of wealthy customers demands a more luxurious setting for its services. While such a setting is feasible, "one-stop shopping" may not be quite so popular as hoped in this income group because sophisticated customers are aware of alternatives and tend to shop around. On the other hand, the concept of the boutique with a personal touch or specialized financial niche in a grand setting may appeal to some wealthy clientele. However, the cost of providing these personalized services will be extremely high for any banking institution.

For the middle class, retail banking may become less personal as electronic banking begins to play a larger role. There will be fewer branch banks and more automated teller machines, automatic bill paying, and deposit of payrolls, extension of teller machines to shopping locations and workplaces, and popularization of pay-by-phone services.

One major problem with retail banking today is that the "spread" or profit is being jeopardized by the soaring cost of obtaining consumer deposits. McKinsey & Company has estimated that the phasing out of Regulation Q could end up costing the banking industry $21 billion annually, an amount equal to the industry's total pretax profits for 1981. A decline in the profitability of retail banking is one of the reasons for the general erosion in the banking industry's return on assets. It should be noted that most good regional banks have higher returns on assets than money center banks because regional banks have traditionally paid less for their deposits than money center banks. Regional banks, on the average, have had less need to purchase funds in the money markets and a much higher percentage of lower cost consumer deposits than their big city counterparts. In order to improve their return on assets, banks have sought to increase their income on pass-through transactions and products and services that are not related to the asset base. This is discussed more thoroughly in a future chapter.

Another problem with traditional retail banking is that costs have jumped by over one-third in a 2-year period. Processing a check at a major bank in 1982 costs approximately 41 cents. Yet, most banks are still charging only 10 to 25 cents for this service. If the banks were to attempt to charge more, they would drive even more of their customers to nonbank competitors, into free *NOW accounts,* or to the use of cash and pay-by-phone systems. By contrast, most money market funds do not charge for checking transactions but limit unprofitable transactions by not accepting deposits under $1000 and offer check-writing privileges with a $500 minimum per check. Allan H. Lipis, president of Electronic Banking Inc., claims that "if banks are going to survive, they must increase their transactional services and decrease their costs. The only mechanism on the horizon for doing that is electronic banking."[3]

Retail banking also faces the uncertainty of deregulation and the rapidly expanding group of new products that NDIs are bringing to the marketplace. While banks are hindered by geographical restrictions and a limitation on services that can be offered, they must still compete with organizations which are both nationwide in scope and have the freedom to offer a comprehensive package of financial services ranging from stock brokerage and margin accounts to quasi-checking.

Of course, retail banking institutions have not been lying dormant. They are laying the groundwork for comprehensive services and are looking forward to the day when a complete package of financial services will be allowed without geographic or interest rate ceiling restrictions, providing industrywide competitive equality. Among the first steps were debit and credit card organizations that permitted wider use of "plastic" to access ATMs. The new money market accounts will eventually combine securities accounts and traditional debit and credit services. Prior to being granted the authority to offer money market fund accounts, some banks offered a "balance sweeping" program to their depositors. (In such programs, balances in excess of a target amount such as $2,000 were automatically invested in a money market fund in increments of $500 or more. Conversely, when the checking account balance dropped to an amount lower than the target, monies were automatically withdrawn from the money market fund to replenish the checking account.) This device helped attract and retain customers while increasing the size of lower-cost core deposits.

Another example of a competitive response to both the NDIs and geographical restrictions is an effort by a major New York City bank to take its retail banking effort coast to coast with selective mailings to professionals. They have offered credit lines via personalized checks and special Visa cards with more extensive benefits than are typically available from competitors. Among additional benefits are the ability to obtain cash at 100,000 banking offices worldwide and emergency cash availability after banking hours and on weekends via a toll-free number and via Western Union offices in over 8500 locations. There is also a "sharebuilder" investment plan that enables one to purchase stocks at reduced brokerage fees, participate in a professionally managed stock mutual fund, or to invest in a money market fund for an initial investment of only $100 and a $1.50 monthly participation fee. The bank also provides a shopper's service for an annual fee of $15 a year, which provides a toll-free call to obtain discount prices for any of over 30,000 brand-name items. Any item can be ordered directly with door-to-door delivery.

Some regional banks have moved to restructure their retail banking services by reducing the number of full-service branches, opening minibranches, and replacing human teller services with automated tellers. In some instances retail market penetration has been increased, while the work force has held steady. Services such as the paying of utility bills, the processing of checks for cash management accounts for brokerage firms, one-day national clearance of checks in select markets, and investment advisory services to mutual funds have added to regional bank profitability. Many regional banks have begun planning for the start of money market funds and discount brokerage. They would like to gain back deposit customers lost to the money market fund industry and to be able to sell their customers shares of stock by debiting the checking account. Some regional banks have invested in other regionals in faster growing parts of the country in an attempt to improve profitability and in preparation for national banking.

Other commercial banks have become more aggressive in bidding for consumer business by using their lending strength to keep big consumer depositors from moving their funds to money market funds. For example, banks have offered car loans at 12 percent if a $5000 minimum deposit is placed in a low-interest savings account. Some banks have offered leased automobiles or other expensive gifts to customers for sizable deposits and multiyear maturities in lieu of interest payments.

Perhaps the greatest effect on retail banking will come from the invasion of electronics. Technological change is propelling the banking industry through the most rapid period of change since the 1930s. Many bank branches are apt to disappear as ATMs and EFTS replace high-cost branch banking. ATMs have become popular in supermarkets, on university campuses, and at hospital sites. Many of the bricks-and-mortar branches in existence today may no longer be needed by the end of the decade and could be leased or sold.

Banks will attempt to become more efficient by cutting costs through mechanization. Although some labor costs will be reduced over the long run, mechanization in the short term serves as a defensive measure to protect against deposit losses in an age of EFTS. There will, of course, be less need for *full-service banks* when a plethora of automated teller machines covers the marketing area. The heavy costs associated with remaining competitive in the face of mechanization will lead to the merger of smaller banks into larger ones. However, smaller banks may not need extensive mechanization if they offer differentiated products which include special personalized services.

Technology will also precipitate fundamental structural changes in the exchange of information and the way products and services are sold, marketed, and priced. While EFTS will be evolutionary with regard to the transfer of money, it will be revolutionary in terms of the exchange of data and information. Totally new marketing systems could emerge. Such systems would provide the consumer with a complete listing of product, service, and price information on a home computer screen. The consumer will be able to purchase goods and services using the electronic media.

Most major corporations and full-service banks have their own computer systems installed. With the hardware in place, the potential exists for corporations to move beyond the current practice of merely mobilizing idle funds to the point of implementing integrated financial management information systems via computer-to-computer linkups among corporations or between corporations and their banks or investment banks.

The progress in telecommunications in recent years has allowed four electronic message-switching services to be put in place—*Bankwire, Fedwire, CHIPS,* and *SWIFT.* These wire-transfer networks are now moving money in minutes and have the capability to transfer funds internationally.

While present systems offer improved speed and accuracy, reduced costs, and better portfolio management (by increasing availability of more information via the system), the establishment of a nationwide link between corporations and their banks lies in the future. Electronic banking—conceived by Chemical Bank as "Corporate TIME" (the Transfer of Information and Money Electronically)—would provide a real-time mode of cash management and batch mode transmission and processing of corporate payment data. In addition, such a system could provide balance histories, target balance projections, and foreign exchange reports. Chemical Bank's Chem Link, a prototype of the electronic banking system, is already in operation.

The extent to which Americans turn to computerized transactions hinges upon the regulatory climate, available technology, and customer acceptance of EFTS. There has been some consumer resistance. Some customers prefer to have checks as receipts for payments made and to control the float. About 70 percent of the families in the United States have checking accounts today, and 55 percent to 60 percent of all adults use credit cards. EFTS have a current market penetration of less than 10 percent. However, by the year 2000, EFTS are expected to reach an estimated 50 to 60 percent of the nation's families, while ATMs are expected to handle over half the transactions in the banking industry by the end of this decade.

However, the ATM is on the threshold of some dynamic new capability as our two national card systems get ready to introduce a dual interchange program allowing a customer from New York to access a bank account from a machine in Los Angeles. According to John F. Fisher, senior vice president of Banc One of Columbus, Ohio, the popularity of ATMs as a delivery system will eventually be replaced by home delivery systems that should begin to appear in the next few years. The delivery of services in the home by the year 2000 will probably be the principal method of consumer banking service. Our society will see a new range of information services available at home that will be as rewarding as the entertainment services delivered today. Personal financial business is likely to be conducted from the home over a voice and data communications phone that may be linked to a home computer and/or TV system.[4] Chemical Bank has introduced a service called Pronto that would allow customers in the New York area to bank at home using personal computers. Customers would be able to keep track of their checking accounts and home budgets, transfer money from one account to another, and pay bills electronically by typing commands on the computer keyboard. Eventually the bank plans to offer electronic keyboard banking services such as the ability to order merchandise electronically, evaluate portfolios, read new reports, check concert schedules, order tickets, retrieve stock quotes, and buy and sell stocks.

Users would need an Atari home computer (the system will eventually be compatible with other home computers and terminals), a television set for a viewing screen, a cartridge similar to a video game cartridge and a device called a modem, which connects the home computer over a telephone line to the bank's computers. In addition to the initial equipment fee, customers will be charged a monthly fee of $8 to $10. Customers would save on postage since they would no longer be writing and mailing checks as the money would be electronically transferred from their accounts to the billing company's account.

Chemical's move is a bit of a gamble because it is not certain that the public is ready to use home computers for banking and because two key banking transactions cannot be performed on the home computer—making deposits and obtaining cash. Chemical will of course offer to license its system to other banks. An important question that must be answered is whether smaller banks will agree to license the system for their own use. If Chemical can convince its correspondent bank network to offer this service to its customers, then the system offers potential for rapid expansion and eventual profitability. However, it must offer a broad array of two-way services, such as airline ticketing or concert reservations, to generate enough customer interest to make the system profitable. Chemical will have lots of competition as the Chase Manhattan Bank, Citibank, Bank of America, a number of regional banks, Merrill Lynch, Shearson/American Express, and Sears–Dean Witter develop their own home banking, investment, or financial service programs.

With improved efficiency of EFTS and the growth of the underground economy (primarily a cash business), the use of checks should greatly diminish. As financial institutions continue to add charges for their services, customers are likely to use EFTS because it might provide a cash savings and save increasingly scarce customer discretionary time. Banks might offer customers a choice of two checking accounts: one in which cancelled checks are returned at a fixed charge; and another in which checks are deducted automatically from an account with no paper and no charge passed on to the customer.

As multipurpose bank cards and EFTS evolve, the following changes could take place:

☐ The National Automated Clearing House will reach maturity primarily as a means of transmitting value earned to the institution designated by the customer. Preauthorized payments will have limited success because they deprive customers of personal control.

☐ As the *automated clearing house* (*ACH*) and bank card movements mature, extensive bank facilities to conduct banking operations will diminish in importance. Reliable, round-the-clock, worldwide electronic access, the interest paid, and the number of consumer options available will become the dominant factors in selecting a financial institution.

☐ The popularity of ATMs and the utility bill payment systems have now been joined by check guarantee services that will feature guaranteeing a check at a *point-of-sale terminal* (POST) location. Point-of-sale proprietary debit cards that allow for the debiting of a creditor account at a point-of-sale location should also increase in usage.

Electronics could permeate other areas as well. For instance, Citibank is using an electronic mail system to communicate with its offices around the country by telephone lines which send "written" messages that appear on a computer screen. Other firms routinely transmit data and information faster and cheaper than by mail or ordinary calls via the GTE Telenet systems.

Apart from this sample, banking has been relatively slow in developing new technology. Legal issues of jurisdiction have been key factors in delaying the use of more electronic equipment. There exists the potential to provide instant execution for just about all types of banking transactions at the customer's home through the use of a leased wire, a telephone, a home computer, or a personal transmitter.

Another future development in retail banking is the use of a *debit card* which allows the customer to make a cashless purchase by debiting his or her bank account at the time of purchase. Interbank, the organization licensing MasterCard, launched Signet, a debit card which allows individuals to have funds automatically withdrawn from their savings or checking accounts. With the acceptance and subsequent growth of EFTS, a nationwide debit card network could appear.

Indeed, if these systems evolve and organizations can communicate directly, one has to question the future of the banking institution as it is known today. There may be less need for banks to act as intermediaries in performing many traditional banking functions.

By no later than 1984, experts predict that most banks will become affiliated with one of six nationally linked electronic banking networks, which will eventually consolidate most retail banking services in much the same manner as Visa and MasterCard unified consumer credit services. These networks will be even more powerful because they will operate with the debit card, which can give access to all of the customer's accounts within a bank. Using an ATM, customers will be able to withdraw cash and make deposits to any account, as well as to transfer funds between accounts and make balance inquiries on a national basis.[5] Before the end of this decade, the services provided by the new networks will be expanded to include electronic funds tranfers from home and retail POSTS (see Figure 4–1).

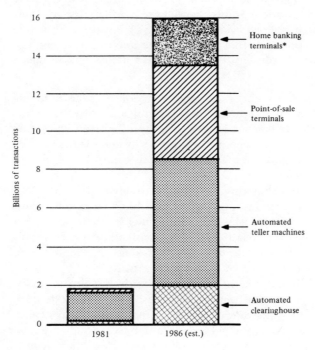

* Includes pay-by-phone systems.

FIGURE 4-1 The growth of electronic payments, 1981–1986. (*Reprinted from the January 18, 1982, issue of Business Week by special permission, © 1982 by McGraw-Hill, Inc., New York, NY 10020. All rights reserved.*)

So far, we have concentrated on the role of commercial banks in the consumer financial marketplace. Now let us look at their depository competitors, the thrift institutions and the credit unions, in the fight for consumer banking business.

NOTES

1 B. E. Gup, *Financial Intermediaries,* 2d ed., Houghton Mifflin Company, Boston, 1982, pp. 394–395.

2 J. H. Wooden, "Banking Industry: Financial Structural Change Monitor," Merrill Lynch, April–May 1982, p. 7.

3 "Electronic Banking," *Business Week,* January 18, 1982, p. 74.

4 J. R. Fisher, "Banking," *Proceedings on The Future of the Financial Services Industry,* Federal Reserve Bank of Atlanta, 1981, pp. 13–14.

5 "Electronic Banking," *Business Week,* January 18, 1982, pp. 70–74.

CHAPTER
FIVE

THRIFT INSTITUTIONS AND CREDIT UNIONS

The first *mutual savings bank* was organized in the United States in 1816. It was patterned after mutual savings banks that were started in Scotland and England earlier in the same decade. The original purpose of mutual savings banks was to encourage thrift among the working-class people. The savings banks invested these savings in the money and capital markets in such a way as to guarantee security of principal and investment. Although mutual savings banks in this country grew rapidly in the northeastern and middle Atlantic states, their growth was restricted geographically. Mutual savings banks generally did not move into the South or West because of either economic conditions or legal restrictions.

Throughout the nineteenth century, the leading occupations in the West and South were agriculture, lumbering, and mining. Unlike the manufacturing and commercial centers of the Northeast, these regions had little need for depository institutions because of the limited number of wage earners. On the other hand, the primary financial need in these states was for credit-supplying institutions like commercial banks.

By the time industrial activity produced a large number of wage earners, commercial banks were in a position to add savings services to the range of facilities already being offered. Another need typically found in the newly settled areas was for construction and home financing.[1]

The earliest *building and loan associations* were organized specifically to satisfy this need. These associations, like the earliest mutual savings banks, were descended directly from English building societies which were a product of England's industrial revolution. Savings associations, like commercial banks, spread throughout the West and South; it was a comparatively simple process for these institutions to add depository facilities as such needs developed. With both building and loan associations and commercial banks providing depository services throughout those regions, incentives to organize mutual savings banks were largely eliminated.[2]

THRIFT CHARACTERISTICS It is interesting to note that the savings and loan industry has grown more rapidly than has the mutual savings bank industry since the mid-1930s. The reasons for this are as follows:[3]

☐ There is a direct and highly significant relationship between local changes in total personal income and the growth of individual institutions.

☐ Mutual savings banks are heavily concentrated in large urban centers where population has been declining and where the average per capita income has been rising less rapidly than in most suburban and other nonurban regions.

☐ Savings and loan associations, having been favored by more liberal branching privileges, are more widely dispersed not only throughout the nation but also in areas of more rapid population growth.

☐ The growth of mutual savings banks was affected by commercial bank competition, as their location forced them to compete more directly with large and aggressive commercial banks.

Savings and loan associations have two distinct forms of ownership. One is the mutual organization in which depositors are owners and are entitled to vote. The other form of ownership is the stock organization, which issues shares of capital stock that can be bought and sold in the marketplace. Shareholders have voting rights and may also receive dividends.

Savings and loan associations may be chartered on either the federal or state level. Federally chartered savings and loan associations are regulated by the *Federal Home Loan Bank FHLB* and are required to have all deposits up to $100,000 insured by the FSLIC. State-chartered associations are monitored by the respective state savings and loan or state banking department. Depository insurance is not required, but most state-chartered associations are insured by the FSLIC.

What are the characteristics of the thrift industry, and how do they differ from banks? According to Professor James L. Pierce, University of California at Berkeley, the thrift industry has the following structural characteristics:[4]

1 Growth orientation
2 Enormous leverage
3 Lack of diversity
4 Dependence upon regulators and Congress for protection from interest rate risk and changing economic conditions
5 Long-term fixed-rate mortgages with yields (on average) below the rates paid for shorter term deposits during 1981 and 1982

Indeed, the investment policies of today's savings and loan associations are oriented toward mortgage acquisition, although a small portion of the portfolio is invested in required liquidity reserves in the form of money market instruments and intermediate-term and longer-term U.S. government securities. Membership in the FHLB and in the FSLIC reinforces this liquidity. Mortgages have become the primary investments of the mutual savings medium with corporate bonds, stocks, and government securities playing a lesser role (see Table 5-1). Many mutual savings banks have recently begun to make commercial and industrial loans to corporate customers as well as installment loans to consumers. Most mutual savings banks are regulated by the Federal Reserve Bank, while their deposits under $100,000 are insured by the FDIC.

THE THRIFT PROBLEM   During 1981 and 1982 thrift institutions suffered through a serious dilemma involving extensive losses related to a mismatched book of assets and liabilities. Essentially, most of these institutions funded their long-term fixed-rate mortgage loans with short-term deposits and money market instruments. The concept of lending long and funding short is not new to savings institutions. However, the combination of a structural shift from relatively low-cost passbook deposits to relatively expensive money market rates paid for deposits during a period of rising interest rates led to considerable

TABLE 5-1
BALANCE SHEET OF MUTUAL SAVINGS BANKS,
MAY 31, 1982, IN MILLIONS OF DOLLARS

	AMOUNT OUTSTANDING	PERCENT OF TOTAL ASSETS
Assets		
Cash and due from banks	5,469	3.1
U.S. Treasury and federal agency obligations	9,968	5.7
Mortgage-backed securities	13,990	8.0
Corporate bonds	16,285	9.3
State and political subdivisions	2,259	1.3
Other bonds, notes, and debentures	3,794	2.2
Mortgage loans	96,334	55.1
Corporate stock	3,417	2.0
Other loans*	17,409	9.9
Other assets	6,027	3.4
Total	174,952	100.0
Liabilities and reserves		
Total deposits	153,354	87.7
Regular deposits†	151,253	86.5
Ordinary savings	47,895	27.4
Time	103,358	59.1
6-month	53,040	30.3
30-month	25,561	14.6
All Savers	6,069	3.5
$100,000 and over	5,199	3.0
Other time	13,590	7.8
Other deposits	2,101	1.2
Borrowings and mortgage warehousing	8,785	5.0
Other liabilities	3,461	2.0
General reserve accounts	9,352	5.3
Total	174,952	100.0

* Includes federal funds, open market paper and other nonmortgage loans.
† Excludes checking, club, and school accounts.
SOURCE; National Association of Mutual Savings Banks.

increases in the cost of funds to these savings institutions without a commensurate increase in yield from the fixed-rate loan *portfolio.* In all instances, the return from the fixed-rate mortgage portfolio was less than the cost of funds used to support it. The extensive shift of funds out of ordinary passbook deposits and into more costly money-

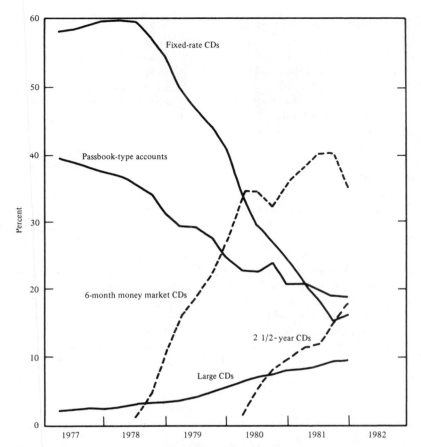

FIGURE 5-1 Decline in savings deposits and increase in consumer CDs in insured savings and loan associations, 1977–1981. (*Source: Federal Home Loan Bank Board. Reprinted in Economic Review, Federal Reserve Bank of Kansas City, July–August 1982.*)

market-oriented deposits of savings and loan associations can be seen in Figure 5-1.

ACQUISITION OF FAILING THRIFT
INSTITUTIONS   The thrift industry suffered many casualties during 1981 and 1982. Among the largest casualties and mergers were the following:

□ The acquisition of the $2 billion Greenwich Savings Bank by the Metropolitan Savings Bank of New York.

- The merger of Union Dime Savings and New York Bank for Savings (both of New York City) as well as the Western New York Savings of Buffalo into the Buffalo Savings Bank, creating one of the largest mutual savings banks in the nation with assets of $9 billion.
- The acquisition by the $14 billion Home Savings of America (the nation's largest savings and loan association) of five ailing Texas thrifts, a troubled Chicago savings institution, two thrift institutions in Missouri, and one in Florida.
- The acquisition by the $7.51 billion California Federal Savings and Loan of three failing savings and loan associations in Georgia and one in Florida.
- The troubled $854.4 million-deposit Farmers & Mechanics Savings Bank of Minneapolis became the first government-assisted merger of a savings bank into a commercial bank, the $239.8 million-deposit Marquette National Bank, also of Minneapolis. The cost of the merger to the FDIC was estimated at $95 million. There had previously been one other consolidation of a savings bank and a commercial bank in 1974 in which Maryland National Bank, Baltimore, acquired the assets and liabilities of the Eutaw Savings Bank of Baltimore. That was different from the F&M-Marquette transaction in that Eutaw was actually closed and its assets and its business were sold off. Another merger between a thrift and a commercial bank involved the merger of Fidelity Mutual Savings Bank of Spokane, Washington, into First Interstate Bank of Washington, Seattle. The estimated cost to the FDIC was $47 million. Dry Dock Savings Bank and Dollar Savings Bank (both of New York City) were merged with assistance from the FDIC. The combined institution will have assets of $5.1 billion.
- *The Federal Home Loan Bank Board* and the Federal Reserve Board approved the acquisition of $3 billion Fidelity Savings and Loan Association of San Francisco by Citicorp of New York. The takeover would be the first acquisition across state lines of a savings and loan association by a bank holding company and might represent a landmark ruling that could clear the way for interstate banking for the entire industry. The Home Loan Board had been under intense pressure from California thrift and banking organizations to turn down the Citicorp bid which was substantially superior to all other offers. The Citicorp proposal would cost the FSLIC $143 million less than the closest competing bid and $302 million less than the FSLIC's cost of operating Fidelity without any takeover. The size of Fidelity's problems made it impossible for the bank board to find a healthy partner within the thrift industry large enough to deal with them.
- The troubled $2 billion-asset Northern California Savings and Loan

Association of Palo Alto was merged into the $10.6 billion Great Western Savings, the nation's second largest savings and loan association.

□ The Federal Reserve Board, in an unusual move, approved the acquisition of Scioto Savings Association of Columbus, Ohio (a state-chartered thrift institution), with deposits of $56.8 million into Interstate Financial Corporation, Dayton, Ohio. Interstate Financial controls Third National Bank & Trust Co. of Dayton (deposits of $471 million), agreeing to operate Scioto as a separate institution and to follow federal interest ceilings that apply to thrifts.

□ The troubled First Federal Savings and Loan Association of Peoria, Illinois, was acquired by Talman Home Federal Savings and Loan of Chicago, just 8 months after Talman acquired North West Federal Savings and Loan Association of Chicago, Unity Savings and Loan Association of Norridge, Illinois, and Alliance Savings and Loan Association of Chicago. The FSLIC extended considerable financial aid to Talman to assist in these combinations. Talman has assets in excess of $7 billion.

□ The Federal Home Loan Bank Board arranged for the merger of Union Federal Savings and Loan Association of Cook County in Matterson, Illinois, into First Federal Savings and Loan of Chicago. That merger was the second involving First Federal during 1982. It previously had acquired First Financial Savings and Loan Association of Downers Grove, Illinois. First Federal Savings and Loan has assets of close to $4.4 billion.

□ The Hartford Federal Savings and Loan Association, which had experienced a run by savers after it reported a hefty 1981 loss, was merged with Schenectady Savings Bank, Schenectady, New York. The arrangement was unusual because Schenectady Savings had to pick up Hartford Federal's charter to become a federal savings and loan association. To accomplish that, the new firm adopted the name Northwest Savings with its main office in Hartford but its administration headquarters in Schenectady. As of December 31, 1981, Hartford Federal had $390 million in assets, while Schenectady Savings had $1.37 billion in assets.

□ The FDIC arranged the merger of U.S. Savings Bank, in Newark, (assets totaling $663 million) into Hudson City Savings Bank in Jersey City (assets totaling $1.3 billion). Hudson City remained the second-largest mutual savings bank in New Jersey following the merger. The FDIC's gross cost will be $65 million; however, if U.S. Savings Bank had been liquidated and the depositors paid off, it would have cost the FDIC $168 million.

□ The Federal Home Loan Bank Board cleared the merger of Knickerbocker Federal Savings and Loan Association, Ninth Federal Savings and Loan Association, and First Federal Savings and Loan Association (all of New York City) into First Federal Savings and Loan Association of Rochester. As a result, First Federal of Rochester will have in excess of $4 billion in assets.

☐ The FDIC arranged the merger of Western Savings Bank of Philadelphia into the Philadelphia Savings Fund Society (PSFS), creating the largest mutual savings bank in the country with assets of $9.5 billion. The cost to the FDIC will be approximately $294 million compared with $696 million if Western had collapsed.

☐ The Erie Savings Bank of Buffalo added more than $1.5 billion to its assets by acquiring three other thrift institutions: The American Federal Savings and Loan of Southfield, Michigan, the Harris County Federal Savings and Loan of Baytown, Texas, and the First Federal Savings and Loan of Mid-Florida, in Delray, Florida. The combination of the four associations gives the new institution, to be known as Empire Savings, $4.72 billion in assets. The FSLIC provided $7 million in cash and issued $52 million in promissory notes to Empire in return for income certificates that will be repaid over time without federal assistance.

☐ Guardian Federal Savings and Loan of Silver Spring, Maryland, was given permission to merge into Perpetual American Savings and Loan of McLean, Virginia. The transaction will combine Guardian's $190 million in assets with $1.8 billion in assets of Perpetual American. The FSLIC provided $10 million in cash assistance to facilitate the merger.

☐ Carteret Savings and Loan of Newark was permitted to acquire River Edge Savings and Loan of River Edge, New Jersey. The merger, which gives Carteret about $2.76 billion in assets, was assisted by $4.6 million in cash from the FSLIC.

☐ First Federal Savings and Loan of Arizona was allowed to acquire Mutual Savings and Loan of El Paso. The acquisition, which required no financial assistance, will give First Federal $2.4 billion in assets.

☐ The FDIC provided $30 million to assist the merger of United Mutual Savings Bank into American Savings Bank, both in New York. Before the merger, American Savings had assets of about $2.5 billion, and United had assets of about $800 million. The combined institution is the fifth largest mutual savings bank in New York State.

☐ The Federal Home Loan Bank Board merged Peachtree Federal Savings and Loan Association in Atlanta and First Federal Savings Association of Crisp County in Cordele, Georgia into Anchor Savings Bank of Northport, New York. The combined institution will have assets of approximately $3 billion.

☐ Garfield Federal Savings and Loan Association in Pottstown, Pa., and Mid-city Federal Savings and Loan Association in Philadelphia were merged into $1.5-billion-asset Horizon Financial Federal Association in Southampton, Pa.
☐ First Nationwide Savings, a subsidiary of National Steel Corporation, was known as Citizens Savings and Loan Association when it acquired two failing east coast thrift institutions in a merger arranged by federal regulators. The merger with West Side Federal Savings and Loan Association, New York, and Washington Savings and Loan Association, Miami Beach, more than doubled Citizens' assets to around $7 billion. Losses from the east coast operations are being covered by the FHLB and the FSLIC, and it is estimated that this assistance would amount to between $131 million and $288 million over the next 10 years. First Nationwide Savings became the country's first interstate savings and loan in September 1981.

The thrifts, of course, have done everything they could, given their large, intractable problems. However, it is anticipated that savings and loan associations will become more dependent on money and capital markets as a source of funds as deposit rate controls are phased out. This could lead to a higher cost of funds and a dominance of variable-rate mortgages offered to the public in order to avoid the interest rate risk of owning fixed-rate mortgages. The thrift industry must become more diversified in terms of the mix of both assets and liabilities and will have to become more profit-oriented and liquidity-conscious if it is to survive. Many of these institutions will in all likelihood operate on a multistate basis because of economies of scale that result from increased size. Out-of-state loan production offices or branches on a regional or national basis will be utilized by the largest and strongest of these institutions.[5]

Some experts foresee a thrift industry with:[6]

1 Some savings and loan associations evolving into one-stop family financial centers or supermarkets that will offer NOW accounts, credit cards, telephone transfer accounts, bill-payer accounts, improved electronic funds transfer services, mortgage and consumer loans, as well as other consumer services
2 Other savings and loan associations offering more specialized real estate services that may emphasize lending to industrial and commercial organizations in the form of short-term construction, acquisition, and development loans
3 Other thrifts emulating mortgage bankers with their focus on secondary market activities, such as the buying, selling, and servicing of

mortgages as a source of profits instead of originating mortgages for addition to portfolio

4 The largest thrifts forming thrift-controlled financial conglomerates that might include, for example, insurance companies, brokerage firms, and mortgage banking companies

Savings and loan associations should look to different kinds of mortgage instruments (discussed later in this chapter) besides fixed-rate loans if sufficient spreads are to materialize over the cost of funds. Whatever the final form, hedging interest rate risks and innovative secondary market trading will be the hallmarks of successful mortgage lending for these firms during the 1980s. Thrift institutions will have to develop lending techniques that enable them to make a profit on their deposits. This will mean offering variable-rate mortgages, personal loans, and loans to businesses that allow short-term deposits to be tied to short-term loans. Also, thrifts may wish to offer fixed-rate mortgages that have a maturity approximately equal to the maturity base of their consumer certificates so that a positive spread can be maintained and the maturity mismatch of assets and liabilities can be avoided.

The problem of failing thrift institutions has been handled so far by the FSLIC and FDIC largely through forced mergers. To assist in the merger process, the FSLIC has sometimes provided cash and promissory notes, indemnified bad loans, taken over unwanted assets, and approved crediting "purchase" accounting procedures. Federal regulators were busy during fiscal 1981–82 attempting to combine ailing and healthy thrift institutions. Analysts expect this trend to continue since it is deemed more economical for the FSLIC than paying off depositors in an outright failure.

Some thrift industry observers believe that the federal government is attempting to cut back on expensive efforts to rescue failing savings and loan associations via assisted mergers and will essentially allow some insolvent thrifts to continue to operate as long as there is no run on deposits. Assisted mergers that do not require much Federal Savings and Loan Insurance Corporation money are expected to continue. The government is expected to issue federal promissory notes permitting mergers of troubled thrifts into each other or into commercial banks that will allow the combined institution to report artificial gains on the transaction. An acquiring savings and loan association can treat the unrecognized loss inherent in the low-yielding mortgage it is taking over as "goodwill." It can amortize the goodwill for up to 30 to 40 years, but income and payoffs from mergers can be taken as income over 10 to 12 years, resulting in substantial earnings from the accounting device. The reason for this change in procedure involves a limited pool of FSLIC funds (estimated at below $5 billion), the enormous expense of "underwriting" a merger, as well as the fact that there are not many healthy thrifts left that can absorb a troubled institution without a great deal of financial support.

If the decision is made to aid a troubled thrift institution through the use of the insuring agencies, then the choice is between paying off the depositors or giving assistance for a merger. A direct infusion of FSLIC or FDIC funds at a nominal interest rate might be helpful in the form of a loan or the purchase of mortgages at par. In either case a deal can be structured permitting the FSLIC or FDIC in a successful turn-around situation to recapture a portion of the benefits accruing to the recipient of the assistance.

By August 1982, the number of assisted mergers in the first 8 months of the year had already exceeded the record of 23 arranged during all of 1981. A Brookings study suggests that over 1000 thrifts can be expected to fail over the next few years while Federal Home Loan Bank officials in October 1982 estimated that over 150 savings and loan associations will be forced into merger or liquidated in 1982, 189 in 1983, and more than 200 in 1984.

There may be some incentive to acquire thrifts. Some commercial banks and healthy thrift institutions are anxious to acquire thrift institutions in parts of the country that offer greater demographic and income potential than the part of the country in which they are currently operating. This was certainly the case in the Citicorp acquisition of an insolvent California thrift institution. This is a step for them toward national retail banking. The cost of acquisition of an ailing thrift has been minimal given the potential opportunity for growth and the assistance from the regulatory authorities. Cost savings are also available through consolidation of accounting, operations, and the closing of the unprofitable branches.

After-tax profits at savings and loan associations rose during most of the 1970s and achieved a record level of $3.9 billion in 1978. Profits turned sharply downward thereafter. In 1981, the industry suffered losses of over $4.6 billion, an amount larger than any year's gains (see Figure 5-2). During 1981, the spread between the market interest rate on mortgages and the return on the average savings and loan association mortgage portfolio had reached 6.7 percentage points, compared with an average of 1 percentage point in the 1971–78 period. Providing another sign of the industry's problems, the number of insured savings and loan associations at the end of 1981 was 211 below the year-earlier total of 4002. The loss reflects the number of mergers

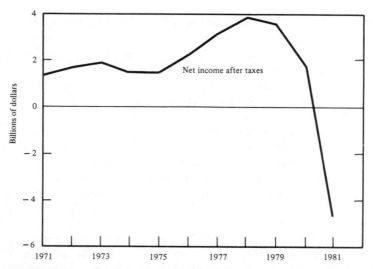

FIGURE 5-2   Income losses at insured savings and loan associations, 1971–1981. (*Source: Federal Home Loan Bank Board. Reprinted in Economic Review, Federal Reserve Bank of Kansas City, July–August 1982.*)

in the industry and, in one instance, the liquidation of a failed savings and loan association in Chicago. Savings and loan deposits rose by less than 1 percent in 1981; the previous smallest deposit gain was 3.1 percent in 1970.

In an effort to further help the ailing thrift institutions and to encourage the flow of funds into housing, the President's Commission on Housing has supported a plan to broaden the power of the nation's thrift institutions. In a final report the panel proposed that the authority of thrift institutions be expanded to strengthen the housing-finance system. It recommended broadening tax incentives for mortgage investment for financial institutions and urged easing laws and regulations that hinder pension funds from investing in mortgages and mortgage-related securities. Federal regulators also approved a new, short-term savings account designed to help banks and thrifts compete more readily with money market mutual funds. By a 4 to 1 vote in 1982 the Federal Depository Institution Deregulation Committee approved a savings account that would require a minimum daily balance of $20,000 and pay interest rates pegged to the Treasury's 3-month bill rate. Thrift institutions could pay the bill rate, while commercial banks would be limited to paying ¼ percentage point less. The term of the account would range from 7 to 31 days. Depositors were not permitted to write checks on the account. This was a step in the direction of deregulation in that it provided institutions with a slightly more competitive short-term account.

In response to the losses experienced by the thrifts, a number of short- and long-run solutions have been implemented or proposed. The short-term solutions—mergers, the use of income capital certificates, promissory notes, and purchase accounting methods—rely in part on low interest rates. Longer term solutions would provide thrifts with the tools needed to become profitable in a wide range of financial environments whether they choose to remain specialized mortgage lenders or whether they choose to compete in other financial markets. A first step along these lines is the approval given to savings and loan associations to make commercial loans and to offer insured *money market fund accounts.*

In addition to being granted money market fund accounts, savings and loan associations are now permitted to invest as much as 5 percent of their assets in commercial loans through 1983 and as much as 10 percent after that. Also, about one-third of the federally insured thrifts should qualify through 1984 for federal assistance. The assistance will be in the form of promissory notes from the FSLIC. Troubled thrifts can use the notes to prop up their net worth (the excess of their assets over liabilities) and avoid being declared insolvent.

Before the aid package passed Congress and was signed by President Reagan, regulators generally started to look for stronger merger partners for savings and loan associations whose net worth fell below 3 percent of liabilities. The new law will prevent them from forcing mergers for institutions with a net worth above 0.5 percent of liabilities. However, the Federal Home Loan Bank Board stated that a number of institutions are too sick to survive even with this aid program. It is estimated that hundreds of savings and loan associations will be forced into merger or liquidation in 1983 and 1984.

Thrift institutions have been given the flexibility to engage in a wide spectrum of financial activities. The variety of financial services includes mortgage lending, commercial and consumer lending, life insurance, brokerage services, and trust management. However, only a small number of thrifts have the strength in management or assets to exploit these emerging opportunities. A few thrifts have moved into these activities and now even operate as interstate and multistate depository institutions.

We are likely to see other changes occurring in thrift institutions that might include:

☐ Increasing yield, the longer the deposit is held

- Permitting these institutions to pay an extra lump-sum bonus on passbooks held for a year
- Creating a new 5-year floating rate certificate similar to the 6-month money market certificate
- Allowing these institutions to invest considerably more of their assets in consumer and business loans
- Allowing new mortgage-backed, pass-through instruments sold in small denominations that would provide a competitive market return to customers, permit the lender to earn servicing fees on the underlying mortgage and free additional funds for lending
- Full commercial banking powers available to thrifts
- Trading financial options on organized exchanges
- Buying and selling of stocks and bonds for customers
- Offering the 6-month certificates in smaller denominations such as $1000
- Operating debt collection services
- Offering real estate brokerage service
- The conversion of mutual savings and loan associations into stock institutions

Although some of these changes might lead to higher interest rates for savers and thus help to hold on to deposits, a higher cost of funds for savings and loan associations implies more red ink. However, many of these devices would offer greater incentives to investors to keep their funds on deposit until such time as interest rates decline and higher profit spreads for thrifts return. Many of the other changes allow additional profit opportunities for these institutions. These changes would also enable savings institutions to compete more directly with commercial banks in the battle for deposits and loans. Without the new incentives being offered to savers, thrift institutions would be at a competitive disadvantage in attracting deposits, especially if consumers lose faith in the depository insurance mechanism.

Adding to the problems of the thrift industry was the collapse of the Penn Square Bank of Oklahoma City. Sixteen federally insured savings and loan associations had a total of more than $16.7 million in uninsured deposits in that bank when it failed. At least one of these thrift institutions is insolvent as a result.

CAN THRIFTS SURVIVE?   Speakers at a Federal Home Loan Bank of San Francisco Conference on the financial environment and financial institutions (December 1981) suggest that even though savings and loan associations have recently been granted new powers that should help them withstand future periods of high and volatile interest rates, the effectiveness of these new powers will be limited by the fact that a high proportion of association assets are embedded in mortgage portfolios. It was suggested that these funds could be released for investment in assets with higher return and/or lower risk through the following techniques:[7]

☐ Offer customers reverse repurchase agreements that could be arbitraged into higher-yielding instruments by the thrift
☐ Make use of mortgage-backed pass-through and cashflow bonds
☐ Arrange for mortgage sales and absorb the resultant tax savings losses
☐ Accelerate mortgage payoffs by existing mortgagors
☐ Reduce the maturity imbalance that exists between asset and liability portfolios by reinvesting in shorter maturities and/or lengthening the duration of liabilities
☐ Increase the use of adjustable mortgage lending
☐ Hedging interest rate risks with financial futures
☐ Issue new savings instruments where interest is paid out only at maturity, e.g., a zero-coupon instrument

Let us see how some of these would work.

Repurchase agreements would generally cost the institutions a rate under the federal funds rate. These funds could be invested in the federal funds market or lent to corporations at about 50 basis points above the federal funds rate. Mortgage-backed pass-through certificates enable the institution to collect, for example, a front-end mortgage commitment fee as well as a small profit or spread on the mortgage interest rate that would be packaged for public sale. They also permit liquidity with the sale of a package of mortgage securities. One could also raise additional capital with mortgage-backed bonds. Thrifts could begin to concentrate on matching assets with deposit liabilities in terms of both maturity and amount at a positive spread rather than having a risky unmatched book of short-term deposits and long-term fixed-rate mortgages at yields below the current cost of funds. If thrifts offer floating-rate mortgages, their yields would always be in line with the thrift institutions' cost of funds. It is also possible to hedge fixed-rate investments against rising interest rates for a modest cost to prevent disastrous losses in earnings during periods of increasing rates. The sale of low-yielding mortgages in the secondary market would provide the institution with much needed liquidity. There would be some tax savings since the mortgages would be sold at a loss and the funds could be reinvested at much higher yields. Under present accounting rules, there is a limit as to the amount of losses that the thrift would be permitted to sustain. However, a one-time change in accounting practices might make this a practical solution for many thrift institutions.

A number of thrifts have encouraged the accelerated payoff of mortgages by existing mortgagors by offering them an incentive. For example, the mortgagor might be offered the opportunity to pay off a $40,000 6-percent mortgage for only $30,000. There can of course be benefits to both parties in this kind of transaction. The thrift gets to reinvest the funds at current market rates which in some cases are at double the old mortgage rate, while the mortgagor saves $10,000. There are also some tax ramifications that are helpful to the thrifts.

In an historic widening of the powers of savings and loan associations, the Federal Home Loan Bank Board authorized them to offer their customers investment and brokerage services. The board had previously approved a plan by a consortium of four associations to form a jointly held subsidiary, called the Savings Association Financial Corporation, that would offer brokerage services and investment advice to the public from offices set up in the lobbies of the participating institutions. Associations participating in the so-called Invest network would execute orders to buy or sell stocks and other securities through representatives registered with the NASD. Ownership of Invest is expected to be broadened to 35 savings and loan associations. An additional 315 have expressed a strong interest in using the service. The move is part of a nationwide trend to provide a one-stop, supermarket type of financial service. Another, complementary, proposal before the Home Loan Bank is one that would pave the way for thrift institutions to sponsor mutual funds, make commercial loans, and even sell real estate through special service corporations. These new powers have been urged in view of losses for the industry of between $6 and $7 billion a year.

Financial futures can now be used to hedge against treacherous interest rate swings. The object of such an "asset hedge" is to guarantee that if interest rates rise and if acquired mortgages consequently fall in value, the thrift can buy back the contracts at a lower price, i.e., paper profits on future hedges would compensate for much of the loss caused by increasing interest rates on the value of newly acquired mortgages. When the contracts expire, the thrift would realize any gains or losses, amortizing them over the life of the mortgages. This has the effect of transforming fixed-rate assets into variable-rate assets.

While the asset hedge allows mortgages to float along with interest rates, its counterpart on the liability side of the balance sheet enables savings and loan associations to fix borrowing costs as far in advance as 2 years. The advantage of liability hedges is to control the costs of borrowing and to minimize the effect of rising interest rates on the cost of funds to the institution. If a savings association is not hedged against rising rates, it may be betting its survival on interest rates declining.

CREDIT UNIONS Thrifts and commercial banks are not the only factors involved in retail banking. Small banks and thrift institutions are being sorely challenged by credit unions for retail banking business. These credit unions are essentially cooperatives in which members pool savings and make loans to one another at reasonable rates. Recently, credit unions have begun to issue share drafts (which are, in essence, checks), credit cards, certificates of deposit, 30-year mortgages, and 15-year home improvement loans. In fact, it would not be inconceivable for credit unions to market their own national credit card that would compete with Visa and MasterCard. At present, some 22,000 American credit unions include in their memberships one-fourth of all households in the United States. While they are generally small operations, several Midwestern credit unions have more consumer assets than all commercial banks and thrifts in their area combined.

Today's credit unions bear little resemblance to the community cooperatives established about 75 years ago to provide the working classes with a place to deposit their savings and a place to borrow money at a reasonable rate. At that time, few commercial banks made consumer loans. Edward A. Filene, a prominent Boston department store magnate, helped establish the first credit union in the United States in order to fill a credit need for factory workers, farmers, and merchants. These savings cooperatives were owned by groups of individuals who worked for the same employer, lived in the same community, had the same religious or club affiliation, or shared some other common bond. To this day, such a common bond usually lowers the cost of collecting and investigating credit information which generally results in a reduction in loan losses.

Today credit unions offer loans on mobile homes and revolving lines of credit, share-draft accounts that pay interest, credit cards, utility bill-paying services, and ATMs. Credit unions are able to provide these services at more favorable terms than most banks or savings and loan associations, while money held in a credit union's share-draft account typically earns more than the passbook or NOW account rate paid by other depository institutions. As a matter of fact, the National Credit Union Association has eliminated all interest rate ceilings (dividends) for federally chartered credit unions. The 12,125 federally chartered credit unions with 2.7 million members join 5000 state-chartered credit unions that have been free from such rate restrictions. The removal of interest rate ceilings gives credit unions a head start over banks and thrifts which may not be released from regulations and ceilings until 1986. They will also have an advantage over money market funds in that they will be able to pay comparable interest rates while offering insurance protection on deposits. Credit unions have another competitive advantage in that they are not prohibited from branching across state lines.

On the other hand, the effect of competitive pressure has led to a slowdown in the growth of savings at credit unions, beginning in late 1978, and a commensurate decline in their share of the consumer installment loan market. ATMs installed in the place of work by banks and thrifts have also eroded the advantages that the credit union has of servicing consumer financial needs in the work environment. Electronic funds transfer and payroll direct deposit programs offered by banks and thrifts threaten the payroll deduction advantages of company credit unions. Many of the smaller credit unions cannot afford the cost of automation needed to remain competitive.

Although many credit unions have had a reduction in earnings, their problems are not as severe on average as the typical thrift institution because they do not have huge portfolios of low-yielding, fixed-rate mortgages. Nevertheless, with the increased competition for funds, the number of people holding credit union accounts has now reached approximately 47 million. The volume of deposits is close to $67 billion, quadrupling the deposit volume of 1971.

RETAIL BANKING AND CONSUMER
MORTGAGE LOANS
Retail banking and mortgages are closely interconnected. Historically, thrift institutions concentrated entirely on retail banking and dominated consumer mortgage lending. With thrift institutions under financial stress and with their new commercial banking powers, savings and loan associations and mutual savings banks may not play as important a role in consumer mortgage lending as they have in the past. A number of new mortgage instruments have been developed in the last few years to attract lenders to this segment of the retail banking market. It is the purpose of this section to explore these innovations.

The emerging trends and demographics suggest an improved outlook for housing through the middle of this decade, particularly if interest rates decline. The demand for mortgage credit could undergo good growth in the 1980s and could be shaped by patterns deviating significantly from traditional ones. However, demographic analysis indicates a peak in the number of mortgage loan seekers toward the end of this decade before a substantial decline in home buying occurs in the 1990s.

Over the next decade there will be fewer fixed-rate mortgages as lenders appear less willing to get into a situation where they are locked into a fixed rate of return over 20 years or more. The fixed-rate loans that may be available will be tied to the maturities of fixed-rate deposits, enabling the bank to make a spread or profit on the loan. This might lead to 3- or 5-year mortgages at a fixed rate that will require renegotiation of the interest rates after the original maturity expires. Lenders prefer variable-rate loans and/or equity participations in the potential capital appreciation of the homes in which they have made a mortgage loan. We are likely to be faced with an array of options in the mortgage market the next time we buy or sell a house that will include *variable-rate mortgages (VRM)*, *graduated-payment mortgages (GPM)*, *shared appreciation mortgages (SAM)*, *growing-equity mortgages (GEM)*, *renegotiable-rate mortgages (RRM)*, *reverse annuity mortgages (RAM)*, and special financial arrangements between buyer and seller during periods of exceptionally high interest rates where affordability of monthly payments becomes a real challenge.

Although these kinds of mortgages generally protect the lender against rising interest rates, the VRM has grown rapidly in importance in California. More than half of the new mortgages in the state are variable-rate. This popularity is more a function of market availability than preference. The VRM's interest rate is tied to an index of the lender's cost of money. It can be adjusted upward or downward every 6 months, but never more than ½ of 1 percent each year, or 2.5 percentage points over the full life of the loan. The GPM, on the other hand, is most helpful for first-time home buyers. It offers a fixed rate of interest that is usually above the market rate but allows the monthly payments to increase along with the homeowner's earning power. The SAM mortgage allows the lender to share in the profit on the sale of a house in return for a lower-than-market interest rate. For example, a bank might offer a 25 percent discount on the mortgage rate for a 25 percent share in the capital gain upon sale of the home. The RRM plan has been compared with the Canadian rollover type of mortgage, which comes due every 5 years and must be renegotiated. The American form is based on a full 30-year mortgage loan contract which the lender is obliged to renew at intervals of 3 to 5 years. The rate cannot be changed by more than a total of 5 percentage points over the life of the loans. Older home owners who have paid all or most of their mortgages and have built up equity in the value of their homes can benefit from the RAM plan, which allows homeowners to tap the built-up equity in their homes. This loan is like a mirror image of the conventional mortgage. Instead of making monthly payments to the lender, the borrowers receive a check each month from the lender for an agreed-upon amount and number of years, based on the equity in their home. The full amount falls due on sale of the home, on a specified date, or upon the death of the borrower. In a growing equity mortgage, called GEM by some lenders, the interest rate is fixed for the term of the loan, but monthly payments go up with inflation. All of the increase in monthly payments is used to repay principal. Pension funds are interested in making these loans because the loans are repaid in 8 to 12 years rather than in 30 years.

Purchase money mortgages, or *wraparound mortgages,* which have been popular in commercial real estate, are also finding their way into the residential market. This is an interesting vehicle whereby the homeowner becomes her or his own banker. In some instances, the buying and selling of a place to live has become more of a commercial proposition than a means of fulfilling a basic human need for shelter.

Not only do we have to deal with the basic high cost of a housing unit, but we will also face mortgage rates that have doubled over the last 5 years. Individuals born during the World War II "baby boom" will find it difficult to buy a home unless the 1981–1982 recession leads to considerably lower housing prices and a drop in mortgage rates. High prices for homes and high mortgage rates are disastrous for first-time home buyers and for those wishing to move to a more expensive home. It will be a great challenge to come up with sufficient capital and innovative, affordable financing to satisfy the basic housing needs that stem from strong demographic factors during the eighties.

So far we have spoken only of retail banking. Let us move on now to wholesale banking which serves the needs of the corporate customer.

NOTES

1 A. Teck, *Mutual Savings Banks & Savings and Loan Associations: Aspects of Growth,* Columbia University Press, New York, 1968, pp. 1–21.

2 Ibid.

3 Ibid.

4 J. L. Pierce, *Conference on the Future of the Thrift Industry,* The Federal Reserve Bank of Boston, October 1981.

5 J. C. Morris, "Look-Alike Financial Institutions Called a Myth," Peat Marwick, Mitchell, Florida Conference, *The American Banker,* September 4, 1980, p. 4.

6 Ibid.

7 "Commentary," Federal Home Loan Bank of San Francisco, Seventh Annual Conference on Strategies for the Future, December 1981, vol. 7, pp, 1–3.

CHAPTER
SIX

WHOLESALE BANKING

Commercial bank managements in the post-World War II period seemed more interested in balance sheet totals than in earnings per share and did not take advantage of the numerous opportunities that arose after World War II. As a matter of fact, it was not until 1957 that the loan portfolios of commercial banks in the aggregate finally surpassed their holdings of government securities.

The 1960s were characterized by innovation among banks and other financial institutions that included the emergence of a number of new money market instruments and the introduction of *liability management* that provided commercial banks with new sources of funds, primarily *"purchased money"* available in large volume at money market rates. The term "liability management," when carried to extremes, suggests that banks no longer needed to provide for liquidity in their asset mix as they could simply "buy" the liabilities that they needed to meet liquidity needs or to satisfy loan demand. With the introduction of certificates of deposit (*CDs*), *Eurodollars,* and the growth of federal funds trading, commercial banks untied themselves from the apron strings of demand and savings accounts. Banks could now turn to purchased funds to satisfy the market's growing appetite for credit.

The decade of the sixties could also be characterized by the integration of financial markets on an international scale and the formation of one-bank holding companies as vehicles for financial services diversification. The 1970s were characterized by increased pressures on the value of the dollar relative to other currencies and gold, the massive recycling of petrodollars, huge loan syndications, and highly volatile worldwide financial markets.

The rapid growth of commercial banking made possible by liability management was a mixed blessing. While effective in meeting rising demands for credit, the rapid expansion of loans and investments in the early 1970s could not continue without proportionate additions to equity capital. The closing of the United States National Bank of San Diego in 1973, followed by the demise of Franklin National and Bankhaus Herstatt further escalated concerns over the soundness of the banking systems in this country and abroad.

The decade of the eighties has so far been accompanied by continued aggressive lending practices by banks in an environment of volatile interest rates and economic stagnation. There has also been a blurring of distinctions between different types of financial institutions and between services offered by the financial and nonfinancial sectors. International credit problems and a number of corporate bankruptcies in the United States, plus sloppy credit practices by a number of major United States banks, which were revealed as a result of the Drysdale and Penn Square failures, have lent further support to the thesis that our entire financial system is quite vulnerable.

Wholesale banking is almost the exact opposite of consumer-oriented banking. Wholesale banking is concerned with loans to domestic corporations, multinational companies, governments, central banks, governmental agencies, supranational institutions, and small and midsized businesses.

Morgan Guaranty Trust Company and Bankers Trust Company are considered prototypes of the wholesale bank. Their portfolios consist primarily of loans to "Fortune 500" businesses and financial institutions, loans to foreign governments and their agencies, as well as loans to major multinational corporations and agencies. Morgan's basic philosophy has called for providing the highest quality of in-depth services throughout the world to only a select segment of the market. Morgan operates with a relatively small number of New York City and worldwide branches, making no effort to saturate the consumer market with installment loans and/or checking or savings accounts. However, it has recently begun to court the middle-market corporate customer.

On the other hand, Bankers Trust began as a "carriage trade" wholesale bank. It then built a huge retail branch system to complement its wholesale banking base, only to sell off most of its branches in the late 1970s and early 1980s. Although it still maintains some of its middle-market business, the bank has decided to concentrate on and provide services to corporations, financial institutions, governments, and high-income individuals. A bank that concentrates on wholesale rather than retail banking avoids considerable personnel costs, huge branch system expenses, check processing expenses, and the costs associated with the extra equipment and computers necessary to process consumer checks.

Successful wholesale banks are likely to have the following qualities:

☐ Flexible enough to provide competitive short-term loans and fixed-rate intermediate-term loans, both at positive spreads over the cost of funds
☐ The pricing of most loans on a "marginal cost plus" or spread basis
☐ Excellent credit quality controls
☐ Sophisticated investment and liability management operations
☐ Excellent foreign exchange advisory and international lending operations
☐ High-quality operational services for corporate customers
☐ Strong sources of income from off-balance sheet, non-asset-based activities and services
☐ The possibility of increased activity under the holding company umbrella that might include factoring, commercial finance, leasing, mortgage banking, and even consumer finance, the last activity being essentially a retail banking function

Domestic wholesale banking has become quite competitive as domestic banks have been challenged by foreign banks, insurance companies, commercial finance companies such as General Electric Credit, as well as the fast-growing, low-overhead *commercial paper* market. The competition offers interesting alternatives. For example, insurance companies have been willing to lend money at fixed rates in the 2- to 7-year maturity range. Life insurance companies, operating in the private placement market, have entered the short- to intermediate-term lending arena because of the availability of attractive rates and because of their desire to shorten the maturity of their investment portfolios which have had a large portion of investments in the longer term maturities. Outside of a modest number of private placements, life insurance company funds have been invested primarily in real estate and publicly traded stocks and bonds. Insurance companies have been successful in generating business away from the commercial banks because they generally offer lower rates, as well as fixed-rate loans without compensating balance. However, insurance companies may not have developed the credit review expertise that most commercial banks have acquired over the years.

Foreign banks have become the discount bankers of the corporate lending sphere, offering cut-rate loans and/or fixed-rate loans in order to penetrate the domestic lending market. Foreign banks have had a cost-of-funds advantage over U.S. banks in that they were able to operate virtually free of capital and reserve requirements. Only recently have foreign banks with branches in this country been required to keep reserves with the Federal Reserve Bank.[1]

Commercial finance companies have concentrated on secure lending activity to smaller and midsized companies where the profit margins on loans are quite high. Finance companies, such as General Electric Credit, have earnings that are greater than the Wells Fargo Bank. General Electric Credit normally offers loans at a fixed spread over the companies' cost of commercial paper—that is, at a rate that is often equal to or less than the prime rate of commercial banks. Few small or midsized companies pay a rate as low as the prime rate at banks. There are also no compensating balance requirements for those companies when they borrow from commercial finance companies.

Finally, the popularity of the commercial paper market is attractive because interest rates are generally lower for qualified borrowers than are rates at commercial banks (see Figure 6-1). The problem with the commercial paper market is that it is not open to all borrowers. It is also wise to remember that the credit problems of Penn Central, W. T. Grant, and the *Real Estate Investment Trusts* (*REITs*) had their origin

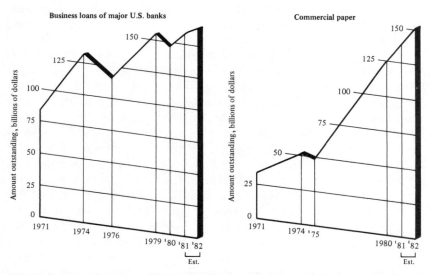

FIGURE 6-1 Growth of commercial paper compared with commercial bank business loans. (*Reprinted from the April 13, 1981, issue of Business Week by special permission, © 1981 by McGraw-Hill, Inc., New York, NY 10020. All rights reserved.*)

in the commercial paper market. These commercial paper borrowings were supported by backup lines from commercial banks which were drawn upon when problems arose.

Reserve requirements, *reintermediation,* expensive branch systems, regulation and detailed reporting to numerous governmental agencies, and depository insurance expenses have raised the costs of doing business for commercial banks. Their cost of funds has also increased substantially. Lower priced loans available from the competition have helped erode the overall credit quality of bank loan portfolios, leaving the banks with a relatively large number of lesser-quality borrowers.

Citing competitive pressures, tax savings, and the prospect of nationwide banking, Chemical Corporation plans to establish a banking subsidiary in Delaware with an initial capitalization of $100 million and says it expects total assets of the subsidiary to reach about $3 billion by the end of the first few years of operation. Chemical Bank joins about nine other out-of-state institutions that in the last year have declared their intention to set up operations in Delaware. The Chemical subsidiary will engage principally in wholesale banking, providing a broad range of domestic and international banking services to corporations and financial institutions. These services will include cash management, real estate lending, and lending to large corporate customers.

Money center banks have attempted to counter the increasingly tougher competition by offering a number of features to generate new income (see Figure 6-2).

☐ Below prime loans for short-term borrowers, e.g., cost-plus pricing of loans based on a modest spread over the federal funds rate
☐ A plethora of new products and services for corporate customers, in return for fees and/or balances, which include:[2]

> Project financing
>
> Arranging leveraged buyouts
>
> Advanced cash management services
>
> Foreign exchange advisory services
>
> Economic services
>
> Security sales
>
> Private placements
>
> Merger and acquisition services
>
> Creative lending
>
> Special-purpose financing for energy development
>
> Multicurrency leases

Providing backup lines for commercial paper issuers

Underwriting for issuers

The challenge now is for banks to create a demand among corporations for special skills, services, and unusual deals because much of the traditional short-term borrowing has been lost. To counter the competition, some banks have begun to offer fixed-rate loans in the intermediate maturity range when they can lock in a positive spread over their cost of funds. Banks have also been offering loans at interest rates under the prime rate. These loans are usually priced at rates between ¼ and ⅝ over the federal funds rate for major corporations who borrow for less than 1 month. To offset these low-profit loans, many banks have attempted to concentrate their efforts for new business on the middle market, where rate spreads are higher than they are for Fortune 500 companies.

The wholesale market is now and always has been a national or international market. It does not matter whether these large customers are serviced by a traveling loan officer or by personnel based in a local loan production office. Since small local banks do not have much or any of this business, any growth in activity in this market by large out-of-state banks has little impact on the local banks.

On the other hand, the middle market is the area in which the growth of interstate banking activity will have the largest impact since

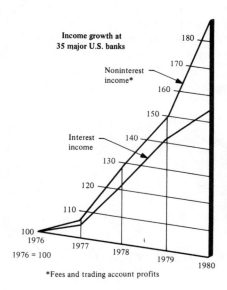

Income growth at
35 major U.S. banks

Noninterest
income*

Interest
income

1976 = 100

*Fees and trading account profits

FIGURE 6-2   Growth of new income sources for commercial loans. (*Reprinted from the April 13, 1981, issue of Business Week by special permission,* © *1981 by McGraw-Hill, Inc., New York, NY 10020. All rights reserved.*)

these firms represent the most prized customers of the local and regional banks. Hence, this is the area in which the conflict between out-of-state and local banks will likely prove most intense. So far, small firms are not yet subject to significant interstate competition. Loan production offices are not an economical device for going after the business of small firms since a deposit-taking facility is necessary to provide full service. Furthermore, making a loan to a small firm without obtaining the deposit account that goes with it is of limited profitability. Also, the higher-priced talent with which a loan production office is staffed means it is not cost-effective to go after small-business lending.[3]

One of the keys to future growth in wholesale banking is cash management products and services, one of the fastest growing areas in commercial banking. Services which enable corporate, institutional, and government customers to expedite the inflow of funds, control disbursements, reduce clerical work, and obtain more complete and timely information are increasing in popularity. Many corporations prefer direct fees rather than balances in compensation for services because they free balances that can be used for investment purposes. They also gain a tax deduction for the fees paid to the bank, constituting a direct business expense.

The quality and breadth of operational services are being given ever-increasing weight by corporate treasurers in their choice of bankers. As electronic payment mechanisms gain wider acceptance, long-standing float management tactics to speed collections and slow disbursements will diminish. And as conventional checks are replaced by electronic impulses, the need for geographically dispersed bank accounts will decrease. Lock-box banking and remote disbursement services will gradually begin losing their appeal.

Because of the sizable initial investment required for computers and communications systems, only the larger and more profitable banks will be able to take a commanding role in these new developments. The big banks could then sell these computer communication systems to their corresponding bank networks or franchises in order to raise fee income and offset costs.

In an attempt to develop additional corporate and foreign lending opportunities, banks have achieved diversification in wholesale banking markets by lending abroad and by establishing loan production offices near domestic corporate headquarters throughout the country. Cities that generate large corporate borrowing have benefited most. These cities include Dallas, Houston, Los Angeles, New York, Chicago, Pittsburgh, and Atlanta. Banks have also established Edge Act Corporations in some of America's chief import and export centers in order to generate additional foreign business. Miami, New York, Los Angeles, and

San Francisco have been among the domestic locations for Edge Act Corporations.

Another way in which wholesale banks have reacted to the competition is to try to generate additional sources of income. Banks have been granting letters of credit to municipalities and housing authorities. These letters of credit guarantee money so that the municipalities or agencies can repurchase the bonds prior to maturity. The banks that are granting the letters of credit generally manage the bond underwritings that the letters of credit guarantee. The legal agreements to issue letters of credit do not require borrowers to retain the banks as underwriting managers. However, it is rare for a bank to grant such a letter of credit without being able to earn the lucrative fees for managing an underwriting.

Other fees could be generated when the legal barriers against investment banking by commercial banks fall. Recent hearings of the Senate Securities Subcommittee have entertained bills to permit banks to expand their securities underwriting beyond the general obligation municipal bonds and housing authority securities that they can now legally underwrite. Some Wall Street analysts believe that making the law more favorable to banks would lead finally to the repeal of the Glass-Steagall Act, which separates commercial banking and investment banking.

Trust income is another source of revenue for many wholesale banks. Many of the nation's financial institutions include the word *trust* as part of their legal name, suggesting fiduciary services. With the passage of the Federal Reserve Act of 1913, which permitted national banks to apply to federal regulatory agencies for trust powers equal to those that state-chartered banks had gained earlier, the fiduciary function of banks has increased enormously in scope and importance. Over 4000 banks offer trust services, acting as administrators and executors of estates for individuals, providing safekeeping custody, escrow, and management services, acting as registrars, transfer agents, dividend disbursing agents, and trustees for corporations managing pension, profit-sharing, and individual retirement accounts. The leading trust banks with the market value of assets under management and the revenue contribution of trust departments to total operating revenues can be found in Table 6-1.

Only three major full-service banks among the top 20 trust banks reported that as much as 6 percent of operating income resulted from trust services (Northern Trust, Provident National, and Wilmington Trust). The fact that the new tax laws offer greater incentive to fund Keogh and IRA accounts and that over one-half million Americans have a net worth in excess of $1 million suggest that trust services, if properly marketed and priced, can become a more important profit-producing component of bank income.

What is the future of wholesale banking? A lot depends on whether banks get back to offering fixed-rate medium-term loans. This is important to their future business because it might lead to the return of a significant amount of high-quality loan volume to the banks. The key to the banks being able to offer medium-term fixed-rate loans is the futures market where interest rate risks can be hedged. Essentially, financial futures open up new opportunities for wholesale banks to fix their costs and to generate additional new lending opportunities at a positive spread.

In the last year or so, government securities dealers, banks and managers of institutional funds have been using treasury bill futures contracts to offset interest rate risk tied to short-term cash market positions. The addition of a CD futures contract has enabled banks to better hedge their liability management positions. It should also allow for arbitraging between the cash market and the futures market. One way for banks to minimize their interest rate risk is to use a liability hedge. When a bank accepts, for example, a 6-month money market certificate, it can almost fix the cost of reissuing a series of such certificates by short-selling securities for future delivery. It can utilize either the futures market for treasury bills or CDs in order to accomplish its objectives. The bank can then lock in a fixed spread by offering a fixed-rate loan if it wishes to continue to price loans on a variable-rate basis.[4]

If banks do not utilize this hedging technique, they run the risk of further erosion of their lending business to the near-banks and the commercial paper market, since insurance companies are willing to lend at fixed rates for intermediate-term maturities and because most borrowing in the commercial paper market is, in general, at rates below those available at commercial banks. Although it has not yet become a severe problem, banks that will not offer fixed-rate loans face the risk of becoming "residual lenders," purveyors of money to companies with low or no public credit ratings and a limited capacity to service debt. In the final analysis, the banks may have reduced their interest rate risk by offering only floating rate loans, but at the price of increasing the risk of defaults by their customers, especially when rates reach extraordinarily high levels. "Banks are now the high-risk lenders in society," according to a Fed official.

Banks will continue to offer their major corporate customers the option of borrowing domestically or in the Eurodollar market. This option enables the corporate borrower to minimize his borrowing costs and allows the bank to lend at a positive spread over either Eurodollar

TABLE 6-1
THE 50 LARGEST U.S. TRUST OPERATIONS, 1981

The 50 giant trust operations below managed over $377 billion in 1981, an increase of barely 1% over 1980. Hindered by a 9% decline in the DJI, 21 of the 50 companies ranked experienced a decline in trust assets managed. Among the top five, J.P. Morgan was down 2.5%, Citicorp down 24.7% and Manufacturers Hanover down 2.1%.

1981 RANK	COMPANY	MARKET VALUE OF TRUST ASSETS* 1981 (MILLIONS)	% INCREASE OVER 1980	TRUST DEPARTMENT REVENUES TOTAL (THOUSANDS)	% CHANGE FROM 1980	% OF TOTAL OPERATING REVENUES
1	J P Morgan	$35,200	−2.5%	$164,294	11.3%	2.4%
2	Citicorp	19,812	−24.7	126,422	15.7	0.7
3	Bankers Trust	19,487	10.2	74,708	17.9	1.6
4	Mfrs Hanover	17,898	−2.1	73,334	14.3	1.0
5	Provident National	15,918	52.5	33,047	25.3	8.4
6	Chase Manhattan	12,528	11.9	88,619	20.3	0.8
7	Continental Illinois	12,458	31.8	53,600	19.6	0.9
8	Mellon National	12,369	−2.1	31,492	11.5	1.4
9	Harris Bankcorp	11,576	7.4	41,878	7.8	4.5
10	Northern Trust	10,767	17.7	58,838	20.5	6.9
11	BankAmerica	10,067	8.6	68,300	12.9	0.5
12	Chemical New York	9,737	7.1	65,072	16.3	1.2
13	Wells Fargo	9,478	3.3	38,713	17.8	1.2
14	US Trust	9,179	−3.9	61,124	16.9	23.6
15	Wilmington Trust	8,515	0.9	14,882	20.8	7.9
16	Crocker National	8,046	−3.0	36,088	15.1	1.4
17	First Bank System	8,001	−3.4	36,692	10.6	2.0
18	First Interstate Bnp	7,455	−13.9	49,152	11.2	1.1
19	First Chicago	6,822	−28.9	45,834	3.7	1.1

22	Bank of New York	6,279	−5.5	93,489	31.0	6.3
23	NBD Bancorp	6,235	−6.5	28,665	2.8	2.1
24	AmeriTrust	6,193	0.2	27,929	3.4	4.3
25	Girard	6,023	26.1	23,903	10.9	4.3
26	Capital Guardian Tr	5,549	−1.7	NA	NA	NA
27	Centerre Bancorp	5,485	0.8	20,406	15.4	3.3
28	State Street Boston	5,168	49.1	38,307	33.4	9.4
29	Northwest Bancorp	5,072	−0.2	31,939	18.7	1.7
30	Republic of Texas	4,597	9.1	25,943	28.8	1.5
31	First City Bancorp	4,594	11.8	17,627	28.1	1.1
32	National City Corp	3,975	−3.4	17,898	23.0	2.9
33	Amer Natl (Chicago)	3,969	−4.4	11,397	7.3	3.5
34	Irving Bank Corp	3,944	12.9	26,307	5.8	1.1
35	Tex Commerce Bshs	3,650	24.2	17,388	27.8	1.1
36	Trust Co of the West	3,506	10.8	NA	NA	NA
37	Citizens & Sthrn Ga	3,461	6.6	10,675	9.7	1.7
38	Fiduciary Trust of NY	3,445	11.4	20,048	24.1	69.5
39	DETROITBANK	3,438	−1.2	18,452	19.6	2.7
40	Boatmen's Bncshs	3,426	3.9	7,424	18.5	3.1
41	Security Pacific	3,309	−22.0	46,596	43.6	1.1
42	Mfrs National Corp	3,288	41.8	11,802	15.6	1.9
43	Wachovia Corp	3,150	2.2	21,330	19.9	3.0
44	Trust Co of Georgia	3,118	0.8	17,856	13.0	4.2
45	Mercantile Bancorp	3,117	0.8	13,210	14.5	2.3
46	First Wisconsin Corp	3,114	−1.7	15,326	14.6	2.6
47	First Pennsylvania	3,061	−3.1	17,709	6.7	2.5
48	Hartford National	3,049	8.0	16,831	14.8	6.0
49	American Fletcher	2,843	0.7	10,052	30.5	2.9
50	Marine Midland	2,812	−9.5	20,987	11.1	0.8

* Includes accounts over which the bank exercises investment discretion.   NA: Not available.

SOURCE: *Forbes*, April 13, 1981, (updated April 12, 1982). Used by permission.

costs or the domestic cost of funds (plus reserve requirements) to the bank. The prime rate should become a dinosaur to Fortune 500 corporate borrowers from banks.

Domestic bank lending will probably be influenced by the events and repercussions of the failure of the Penn Square Bank and Drysdale Securities. There will probably be tighter credit controls and less desire to rapidly expand loan volume without appropriate measures of quality control. The United States does not hold exclusive rights to bankruptcies and problems of credit quality as can be seen by the well-publicized problems of Dome Petroleum, Massey Ferguson, AEG Telefunken, and Banco Ambrosiano, Mexico, Argentina, Brazil, and Poland. Many wholesale banks generate a large portion of their earnings from foreign lending activities. Let us begin our discussion with some history and a summary of current trends.

International lending has a long and important history, including loans to governments by international financiers such as the Fuggers in the fifteenth century and loans to help finance international trade and commerce by the Dutch during the seventeenth century. During the Industrial Revolution, the accumulated capital from trade and expanding industrial production was effectively mobilized and lent by the British to foreign governments, industries, and commercial enterprises throughout the nineteenth century. The outbreak of World War I marked the rise of both New York as a leading financial center and the United States a a major international creditor. More recently, the accumulated wealth of some OPEC members has helped to change the role of debtors and creditors in international lending,[5] as well as some risk-reward relationships, particularly in assessing loans to non-oil-producing and developing nations.

The development of the money and capital markets of Wall Street following World War II helped New York City challenge London as the financial center of the world. The advent of the European Common Market in 1958 led to the revival of the international financial markets in Europe, while the growing desire for economic development in Asia, Africa, and Latin America during the 1960s and 1970s resulted in an increase in syndicated Eurocurrency loans and an increase in the importance of Asian financial centers. Another impetus was the desire by U.S. banks to expand profit opportunities and avoid regulatory control. Banks are not restricted in most foreign countries from the underwriting of corporate securities as they are in the United States.

There were several important and noticeable developments in international lending during the 1960s that influenced the stream of future events:[6]

- Western Europe and Japan became partners with the United States in sharing the financial burden of assisting the developing nations.
- The industrial countries encouraged private industry and banks to become multinational in scope.
- The growing importance of international financial institutions and the Eurobond and Eurocurrency markets acted as a catalyst in contributing to the mobility of international capital on a global basis.

American banks pioneered the trend toward international banking by following American multinational firms into Europe after World War II, helping to establish a Eurodollar market. However, banks are beginning to look beyond the Eurodollar market for profits because:

- The maturity, increased competitiveness, and slim profit margins of the Euromarket make it less attractive today than previously.
- The market's OPEC participants, with the exception of Saudi Arabia, have learned to handle their own money, breaking away from their earlier heavy dependence on Western banks.
- Bank customers "shop around" and no longer assume that their traditional banker can best meet all their needs.
- Major multinational corporations have set up their own foreign exchange dealing rooms, thereby avoiding the banks.
- The growth of a wide range of near-banking activities, e.g., merger and acquisition searches, leasing, investment advice, management services to foreign governments, and more barter activity.

European banking markets have grown at attractive rates in the decade of the seventies because of the explosion in inflation, interest rates, and debt. These markets have been dominated by the large German, English, French, Italian, Swiss, and American banks. The non-American giants have, on average, become more powerful, more competitive, and more willing to assume risks in the last few years. American banks have lost market share and their dominance of the Euroloan syndication market, although they remain an important factor in the wholesale Eurodollar market. With the exception of the European penetration of the banking markets in the United States, the Middle East, Asia, and South America and with the exception of a number of new banking services and products, the main business of continental banking has remained in the lending sphere.

So far, new products and services, technological advances and systems improvements have had little impact on the basic economics of

European banking. The reasons range from nonuniformity of check sizes in France to complete resistance to back-office automation in some countries. This is related to political factors, union power, and lack of profit incentives which are tied to social regulations. Finally, most bankers believe that any significant breakthroughs in technology affecting banks will take place slowly and will affect all players equally. The result will be that no competitive advantage will be derived by those who are pioneers.

European banks are also working on improving their systems capability in order to catch up to American banking standards in the computer area. European retail bank customers have less need for automated teller machines and cash in general than American consumers because of fundamental institutional differences between European and American payment systems.

The range of international banking services varies considerably from bank to bank, whether in this country or in the rest of the world. The degree of sophistication of international services offered depends upon location, size of bank, marketing area emphasized, and field of expertise. However, as a general rule, certain minimum basic services such as lending, extending other forms of credit, handling international payments, collections, letters of credit, and foreign exchange tend to be available at almost all commercial banks that provide international services. New techniques and obligations that have been developed over the last two decades include the issuance of medium-term notes; floating-rate bank loans, notes, and bonds; leveraged buyouts; Euroborrowings in dollars and foreign currencies; lease financing; and original-issue discount bonds (including zero-coupon bonds). American corporations are arranging bank loans which incorporate the option to switch interest rate calculations from a LIBOR rate base to the prime rate base, or vice-versa, on rollover dates of every 3 or 6 months. Hedged transactions have become increasingly important in international money markets as investors routinely compare the return in hedged Canadian dollar instruments, for example, with that in comparable U.S. dollar instruments. One of the salient trends in the decade should be the inclination and ability of international market participants to create custom-tailored synthetic vehicles, by combining instruments denominated in one currency with foreign exchange swaps or contracts or even interest rate futures.

The growth of international business will likely continue, including foreign trade, direct investment, and portfolio investment transactions. This will generate an increased demand for international financial services. The large number of mergers and amalgamations of existing foreign banking institutions is also likely to continue. Just as in the

United States, competitive pressures in international banking had led to declining spreads on loans. However, recent international credit problems appear to have restored spreads to a more normal risk-reward relationship.

What changes lie ahead?

1 A possible structural change in branching practices of banks in Europe has been occasioned by technological advances such as Prestel, an English home TV attachment that makes it possible to conduct banking at home. Visual display formats and telephone linkages allow Prestel users to "shop" and "pay" for products and services at home by transferring debits and credits through a keyboard attached to the television or through verbal telephone messages. Users of this *pay-by-phone* service are able to apply for a loan or obtain a television screen printout of a store's catalog, enabling the user to initiate purchases through the terminal and to debit a bank account. Both American and German companies have purchased rights to this technology in their respective countries. So far, telephone systems in the United States have been directly linked to bank computers to conduct retail banking business without direct contact with the store where the purchase would be made. Automated teller machines in the United States have extended the retail banking function to a 24-hour, 7-day per week operation at supermarkets, places of work, hospitals, college campuses, and at locations adjacent to the bank branch.

2 The worldwide banking giants will continue to expand, while many medium-sized and small banks will disappear through merger or failure. As in the United States, there will always be room for the small specialty shop that will fill profitable voids in the marketplace. However, competition will be tough in the few remaining specialized segments of the financial industry. The growth rate for European banking on the continent will slow down as financial markets in Asia and South America expand more rapidly.

3 American banks are facing growing competition from foreign banks in the pursuit of wholesale business. The United States has become a more important wholesale and retail market to European banking interests. The number of foreign banks operating in this country is increasing because of the ease of entry into the lucrative American marketplace both from a regulatory and cost-of-acquisition viewpoint. Foreign banks also have a distinct "regulatory" and geographic advantage over most American banks. They are subject to less regulation and can operate in more than one state. The investment in American plants by foreign companies such as Sony and

Volkswagen has also encouraged foreign banks to open offices in the United States as a means of following their customers. A number of European banks have purchased major U.S. banks in California and New York.

4 Capital should continue to flow through and toward the Americas and Southeast Asia as a result of:

☐ Economic stagnation in parts of Europe
☐ Macroeconomic and political change, as well as international currency dislocations that have affected the direction of flow of European funds
☐ The rapidly expanding role of government in the financial community and the private sector as a whole
☐ The growing demand for capital in developing countries

5 Pressure has been placed on governments to become directly involved in financial intermediaries because of public desire to provide limited banking services to persons of modest means and improve allocation of funds within the capital markets. This has led to the state takeovers of private financial institutions and to the creation of new public financial intermediaries. Government intervention in the capital markets has occurred as a result of a drop in gross private savings and investment in seven out of nine European countries between 1960 and 1980.

6 The movement to politicize banks will persist during the 1980s in an effort to meet national political objectives and to finance projects that are losing huge sums of money under the guise of government efforts to maintain employment. Consequently, some banks have limited freedom of choice and have suffered liquidity and asset quality deterioration. If this declining trend in bank capital as a percentage of total assets continues, the private market approach to banking could diminish. Under this scenario, government-owned and -managed commercial banks would consequently have significantly greater growth. On the other hand, financial deregulation and monetarism among central banks have been in vogue in certain key countries of late. Credit market barriers among institutions and among countries have been particularly dismantled through floating exchange rates and the pricing mechanism.[7]

7 Changes in international banking regulations are having an important effect. For instance, the relaxation of restrictions upon these banks could allow Edge Act Corporations to:

☐ Extend loans and accept deposits from customers having two-thirds of their purchases or sales directly related to foreign trade

☐ Finance the production of American goods designated for export (formerly limited to the shipment and storage of these goods), enhancing bank flexibility in financing U.S. exports

☐ Establish domestic branches

With domestic branches permitted, a bank could consolidate its Edge Act Corporations into a single entity with a lending limit determined by a larger capital base. Edge Act Corporations would become more competitive with foreign banks in major credit transactions. In addition, a wider range of smaller banks could become involved in foreign trade financing.

8 The emergence of instability in the world financial markets has changed the role of banks in the credit intermediation process and has shifted maturity structure in the capital markets. Interest rate volatility has driven credit demands from the longer-term to the shorter-term markets and has altered the investment decisions and savings patterns of individuals. In the United States, the role of commercial banks in the domestic economy is becoming more important, particularly since other depository institutions (thrift institutions) are experiencing serious liquidity and profitability pressure. Also, high long-term interest rates and the scarcity of long-term fixed-rate investment dollars have forced some borrowers to become increasingly dependent on bank credit.[8]

9 It is highly questionable whether the rewards in international banking justify current credit risks. Over the last 10 years we have seen the profit spread on the London Interbank Offered Rate (LIBOR) that sovereign borrowers must pay in the Euromarkets fall from an average of almost 200 basis points in the 1974–75 period to as little as 37.5 basis points recently.

10 In the future, it will be interesting to see in which countries money market funds will develop, given their success in the United States. In Germany, the Bundesbank has resisted the development of deutsche mark CDs and money market funds, preferring conventional bank deposits as the principal short-term instrument in the domestic deutsche mark market. We should eventually see the development of deutsche mark denominated CDs, either de jure, with official blessing via deregulation, or de facto, as market participants create their own instruments by combining a currency hedge with CDs denominated in some other currency. After all, banks in Luxembourg paved the way in introducing more flexible deutsche mark vehicles. The trend toward deregulation has taken hold in Japan where competitive interbank markets in call money and *Gensaki* have been allowed to develop, as has an active retail market in

yen CDs. Foreign exchange controls have been relaxed, allowing Japanese insurance companies and pension funds to diversify some of their assets into international markets. England is also ripe for a dollar-denominated money market fund.

11 A number of adventurous bank holding companies are setting up export trading subsidiaries that will allow them to earn fees by helping to expand exports of small and medium-sized U.S. customers that lack the resources to pursue overseas sales. Trading, besides earning profits, should generate an added flow of traditional international banking business such as financing letters of credit, and collection services. Only a few banks are expected to enter into this nonfinancial activity since most banks do not have much spare capital now. Many banking institutions would rather use their available capital to expand into areas closer to their main-line business and avoid the risk-oriented world of export sales, barter, and countertrade.

NOTES

1 P. M. Horvitz, "Geographical Restrictions on Financial Institutions," *Proceedings on The Future of the Financial Services Industry,* Federal Reserve Bank of Atlanta, 1981, p. 44.

2 "Wholesale Banking's New Hard Sell," *Business Week,* April 13, 1981, pp. 82–84.

3 Ibid.

4 S. Rose, "Banks Should Look to the Future," *Fortune,* April 20, 1981, pp. 185–192.

5 A. Angeline, M. Eng, and F. Lees, *International Lending, Risk and the Euromarkets,* John Wiley & Sons, Inc., New York, 1979, p. I.

6 F. Lees, *International Banking and Finance,* John Wiley & Sons, Inc., New York, 1974, p. 370.

7 H. Kaufman, "Banking in the Changing World Credit Markets," *Symposium on a Challenging Future for Banking,* Luxembourg, November 1981, p. 1.

8 Ibid., p. 2.

CHAPTER
SEVEN

INVESTMENT BANKING AND BROKERAGE

Investment banking received a late start in this country because of the primitive nature of the American economy which was 90 percent agricultural in the eighteenth century. Most transactions were handled on a barter rather than on a money basis. Another reason for the slow development of American banking lay in the fact that the creation of credit was dominated by English suppliers of capital funds since most foreign trade took place with England. The American merchant who obtained credit offered it to his customers, carrying on a banking business as a sideline to merchandising. Some merchants became private bankers dealing in something more than commercial banking, but less than *investment banking.* They dealt in long-term credit, foreign exchange, bills of exchange, and securities.[1]

Thomas A. Biddle formed the first *investment banking house* in the United States in Philadelphia in 1764. Alexander Brown left his dry goods business in Baltimore and set up another investment bank in that city. Other merchants and general store proprietors who had been advancing credit to their customers in domestic trade joined the transition from selling goods to selling credit. They would include, among others, Lehman Brothers, Goldman, Sachs & Company, Kuhn, Loeb & Company, Astor and Sons, and Corcoran and Riggs.[2]

In the early years, private bankers did little investment banking or securities underwriting. American investment banking remained a small and precarious business until long after the Civil War for the simple reason that raw materials for a securities business did not exist in abundance. Even government securities were in short supply.

The investment banking community, best known for their ability to underwrite and distribute new corporate debt and equity issues, and the brokerage community, best known for their buying and selling of stocks and bonds, have gone through a rather turbulent period over the last two decades. The turbulence has been related to changing economic conditions, collapsing markets, new competitive conditions, and in some instances, poor management.

Historically, according to Samuel Hayes, Jacob Schiff Professor of Investment Banking at the Harvard Business School, access to large amounts of high-quality securities "product" has been vital to the retail distribution firms.[3] While these firms enjoyed strong buyer loyalty from their retail investment customers, their heavy costs for branch office networks, communications systems, and back-office facilities made them depend on high levels of volume. When the equity markets collapsed in 1969–1970 and interest rates soared, originating underwriters found themselves dependent on the retailers to sell the debt securities which their corporate clients urgently wanted to place. This role reversal altered the balance of power in traditional syndicates.

Many large firms decided to "go public" in the early 1970s, replacing insider funds with public investors' money. As losses appeared within the investment banking industry during the economic malaise of the period 1973–74, and after May Day 1976, some firms faced the threat of hemorrhage of their capital through withdrawal by older or inactive partners concerned over the safety of their principal. There was also the need to make back-room operations more efficient.

Other elements of institutional and structural change have made it more difficult for investment bankers and brokers to maintain their profits:

☐ Negotiated rates for institutional business.
☐ The quantity and quality of financial staff resources in the largest U.S. corporations have grown impressively in recent years.
☐ The partial elimination of the investment banking underwriter in corporate "Dutch auctions," in the direct-issue commercial paper market and in shelf registrations.
☐ Temporary unfavorable shifts in the mix away from more lucrative equity financings toward thinner-margin debt offerings also hurt

the industry in 1974 and 1977. This was a function of credit conditions as well as a product of the marketplace.
□ The growth of discount brokers.

The investment banking industry is in the midst of an important transformation. The adverse impact of inflation upon operating costs, coupled with the elimination of fixed rates, has driven many firms from the business since 1970. Successive waves of mergers and liquidations have significantly raised the level of concentration in the industry. Membership in the Securities Industry Association has fallen from 850 in 1972 to approximately 500 in 1982. The survivors are much larger institutions with broader capital bases.

The classic investment banking segment of the securities business is going through a period of upheaval and transition. Commercial banks and insurance companies are threatening some parts of the business through the underwriting of revenue bonds, the purchase of discount brokerage firms in the case of banks, and the outright acquisition of securities firms by insurance companies. Traditional corporate underwriting relationships are being tested, challenged, and fragmented.

Because of negotiated rates on institutional trades, institutional commissions have suffered. The mix of revenues has changed over the last 10 years as the share of securities firms' revenues from brokerage commissions shifted from 60 to 40 percent. Even the retail commission business has suffered from competition from small regional discount brokers. The retail commission business has also been buffeted by a raging war for top sales personnel that has brought higher cost of retail production. However, retail commission rates have increased at the nondiscount firms, possibly producing higher income for these firms.

The investment banking revenue mix has lagged and has moved away from corporate underwriting toward private placements as well as toward highly profitable corporate fee services and municipal finance activities. The wave of municipal finance underwriting in recent years has led to the assignment of more staff to research, consultation, and new business development in the municipal area. An extremely profitable segment of the municipal business has been revenue bonds issued to finance projects ranging from pollution control to hospitals.

Brokerage firms have also begun to develop and market their own mutual funds, money market funds, real estate, and tax shelters during this decade in order to find additional sources of revenue. Investment bankers also entered the commercial paper and Eurodollar markets as financial intermediaries. The growth of these markets has provided

TABLE 7-1
MERGER AND UNDERWRITING INCOME FOR SELECTED INVESTMENT BANKERS IN 1981

COMPANY	VALUE, IN THOUSANDS OF DOLLARS	TRANSACTION AND DATE	INVESTMENT BANKER	FEE, IN MILLIONS OF DOLLARS
Du Pont	7,214,853	Acquisition for cash and common stock; September 30, 1981	First Boston	15
Conoco			Morgan Stanley	14
Fluor	2,342,945	Acquisition for cash and common stock; August 3, 1981	Lehman Brothers	5
St. Joe Minerals			Smith Barney First Boston	
Standard Oil of Ohio	1,767,592	Acquisition for cash June 4, 1981	Goldman Sachs	NA*
Kennecott			Morgan Stanley	0.75
American Telephone & Telegraph	1,034,500	Offering of 18,150,000 shares of common stock; June 10, 1981	Morgan Stanley Goldman Sachs E. F. Hutton et al.	28
Federal National Mortgage Association	1,000,000	Offering of 15% debentures due 1983; September 10, 1981	Various dealers	1.25

* Not applicable.

a new source of earnings to participating institutions. Merrill Lynch has gone a step further than most of the investment banking competition by forming its own international bank which takes credit positions and acts as an underwriter in Euroloan syndications.

Some investment bankers provide extensive merger and acquisition services (see Table 7-1) as well as other corporate financial and counseling services. More recently, a number of the wholesale firms have started in-house brokerage activities aimed at wealthy individuals, whose needs often compare in size with those of the smaller institutional investors. The aim is to provide personalized financial services including insurance and quasi-banking activities to wealthy retail customers.

Companies like Sears–Dean Witter, Shearson/American Express, Prudential-Bache, Merrill Lynch, and others may be able to use their large capitalizations to advantage in enlarging and integrating services for the governmental, corporate, and institutional sectors, as well as increasing their penetration of personal lines of insurance.

Although the investment banks now have the upper hand on fee services, this lucrative area seems vulnerable to a squeeze in margins from several directions. The prospects of falling margins loom in the municipal revenue bond area as the field of intermediaries becomes more crowded. It is also likely that there will be increased competition in the merger and acquisition business. Expertise outside the investment banking business, such as management consulting or the consulting arms of commercial banks, is beginning to make its presence felt in these lines of business.

The likelihood is for continuing profit pressures, both indirectly through the fielding of more extensive corporate services and more directly through such vehicles as the further proliferation of comanagership. There will probably also be assaults on the gross spread or increased pressure to price aggressively. If corporations succeed in transforming certain types of debt offerings into a quasi-commodity business, they may eventually hire an investment banker as financial adviser for an issue and run de facto competitive bidding for the issue.

Also, on February 24, 1982, the *Securities Exchange Commission* (*SEC*) adopted Rule 415 on an experimental basis for a 9-month period. The new rule could completely change corporate underwriting techniques since the "shelf registration" process provides a mechanism for employing new options in both the timing and pricing of securities.

Corporate issuers will be able to file one or more shelf registration statements covering an aggregate amount of securities reasonably expected to be sold within the next 2 years. Once effective, the shelf prospectus can be used for single or multiple offerings through the mailing of a prospectus supplement to the SEC after the pricing of any, or all, of the registered securities. The process provides issuers with an opportunity to price and offer securities instantly—size of offering, maturity, price, and spread can be set at any time without any delay for SEC review. Issuers should be able to move efficiently; cope with the market's volatility and constantly changing investor preference through speed of issuance; customization of terms; and flexibility of offering size, type of security and format of underwriting. Rule 415 specifies that the issuer may designate one or more potential managing underwriters in the shelf filing. As long as one of these underwriters is selected as manager or comanager for a particular underwriting, the offering can be priced on an instantaneous basis by means of the "sticker" supplement to the effective registration supplement.

It is expected that insurance companies and banks, through their merchant banking subsidiaries, will attempt to bid directly for these debt instruments. The winning bidder will have the option of holding the bonds in their own investment portfolio, or placing them in their trading account for eventual secondary market sale. Eventually, banks and insurance companies would like to have corporate underwriting privileges. The entry into this field by banks and insurance companies is a distinct threat to the profitability of investment bankers that concentrate on the underwriting of corporate issues. These large intermediaries consider that Rule 415 will enable them to establish a closer rapport with the corporate treasurer for decisions that will impact future bank loans and risk management plans.

SEC Rule 415, which allows corporations to sell securities directly to investors, poses a threat to many of the prestigious investment banking firms that are dependent upon corporate underwritings for a large share of their income. Many corporate clients would prefer to see their stock widely distributed among individual investors by an underwriting with a network of hundreds of branch offices, rather than held by a few large institutions, who often dump stock on the hint of such bad news as an earnings decline. Morgan Stanley, Goldman Sachs, First Boston, and Salomon Brothers, primarily underwriters with institutional sales forces, could be adversely affected by this new SEC rule. Investment bankers are worried about the potential decline in corporate underwritings associated with Rule 415 which would cut underwriting profits and possibly harm regional securities firms.

Investment bankers are adapting to a new state of affairs: wide-open price competition for underwriting stocks and bonds has dropped fees to extremely low levels. There have even been a number of "bought deals," a European technique in which one or a few investment bankers usually buy the entire offering without lining up buyers in advance and attempt to resell the stocks or bonds at a profit. A number of utility-stock offerings have been handled as bought deals, bypassing many regional security firms that once were members of underwriting syndicates that formerly distributed these securities to the public. National stock and bond offerings had been an important source of merchandise and profits for regional brokerage firms who dealt mostly with local individuals. Shelf registrations and "bought deals" should favor investment bankers with the most capital and the best trading operations.

Companies could also start selling registered securities directly to investors, particularly institutional investors without any underwriters participating. Even when the underwriters are involved in distributing corporate securities, investment bankers may be working for rather low fees.

As an example of a shelf-registration deal, Exxon Corporation announced plans in May 1982 to raise as much as $500 million in company-guaranteed debt securities under the Securities and Exchange Commission's new Rule 415. This allows a company to issue securities "off the shelf," without further disclosure, once the initial filing has been made. The external financing will be the first Exxon debt issue in this country since 1976. The securities will be of 3- to 5-year maturities and are novel because they will be sold in the United States in either bearer or registered form and will also be simultaneously available for foreigners to buy overseas. Issued by Exxon Finance, a Netherlands Antilles entity, the securities would not be subject to withholding taxes for foreign investment (see Table 7-2).

As part of their response to SEC Rule 415, Morgan Stanley has

TABLE 7-2
SELECTED SHELF REGISTRATIONS, 1982

ISSUER	FILING DATE	SECURITIES REGISTERED UNDER RULE 415
Texaco Producing	October 21	$500 million debt
Kidde	October 21	$200 million debt
Niagara Mohawk	October 21	$100 million first mortgage bonds
Atlantic Richfield	October 18	$400 million debt
Security Pacific	October 18	$150 million debt
Exxon Finance	May 5	$500 million debt
American Telephone & Telegraph	April 27	10 million shares common stock
Du Pont	April 2	$ 1 billion debt

teamed up with Kleiner, Perkins, Caufield, & Byers, a successful West Coast capital investment firm, to raise $150 million from largely institutional clients. The incentive for Morgan Stanley is the desire to identify emerging growth companies that could be future underwriting clients. Dillon Read & Company and L. F. Rothschild, Unterberg, Towbin, among other investment firms, have recently set up their own venture capital funds. Morgan Stanley and Dillon Read, major corporate underwriters, have been hurt by SEC Rule 415 which has reduced earnings from corporate underwritings. They are expected to become more active in handling private placements of debt for young companies and eventually doing corporate underwritings when these young companies mature and require an investment banker.

Another innovation is Merrill Lynch's plan to offer its Sharebuilder discount securities program through the branches of two major New York City banks. According to a Merrill Lynch spokesman, the Sharebuilder account is now used by more than 400,000 customers and is offered in the brokerage firm's 395 offices around the world. Current participants in the Sharebuilder program inform Merrill Lynch which securities they want to buy. The purchases are pooled each day, making it possible for the brokerage firm to offer discounts of 15 to 50 percent. The investor could find that bad executions or obtainment of a suboptimal stock price could offset the lower commission.

The plan carries a maximum investment of $5000, limiting it to middle-income consumers who are likely to make small stock purchases. A wide range of stocks can be purchased through the program, including all securities listed on the New York and American Stock Exchanges, plus 700 other stocks regularly handled by Merrill Lynch. If this practice becomes adopted on a nationwide basis, it poses a serious challenge to the nondiscounters in the retail market. For Merrill Lynch, the largest broker, the success of its discount operation would transform it drastically from a retail to a discount brokerage firm.

Although the discount brokers captured only about 10 percent of all retail brokerage commissions in 1981, their market penetration is expected to grow rapidly[4] because of the basic desire on the part of investors to buy stock with the lowest possible commission price and because of their affiliations with commercial banks. The move by Fidelity Management and Research Inc., the Boston-based mutual fund house, to open its own discount brokerage subsidiary could have a powerful impact on changes in the retail sales effort. Bank America's purchase of a discount broker suggests greater competition for the retail account and seems to ensure the continued growth of retail discounters.

Another development is a Chase Manhattan Bank financial planning service to brokers, insurance companies, and banks. The Chase Plan would provide client companies with computerized financial information which they can offer in turn to their customers. The financial information would be available on computer terminals, into which brokers and other financial advisers could enter a customer's financial profile. They would then receive general financial advice on whether the customer should invest, for example, in stocks, tax shelters, or municipal bonds. Chase is also offering discount brokerage arrangements and access to a money market fund through Merrill Lynch. Chase will receive a monthly fee from its customers for this service.

On the retail level, the Chase Plan is sold to corporations as a financial advisory service to their executives as part of an employee benefit package. On the wholesale level, the plan is marketed to brokers, trust departments, and other financial institutions that will use it to make recommendations to their customers about their investment strategies.

An area of great uncertainty and concern is the prospect of greater commercial banking involvement in both brokerage and investment banking. Regulatory barriers were ineffective in preventing the Chemical Bank from launching a short-lived discount securities brokerage operation. Regulatory barriers have, so far, prevented commercial banks from underwriting revenue bonds, but this is being challenged by the banking lobby. The major commercial banks have developed strong investment banking capabilities overseas in underwriting bonds, syndicating loans, and facilitating mergers and acquisitions.

If commercial banks were to obtain regulatory approval for national branch banking, the securities industry might be allowed to perform depository functions for consumers. A number of retail firms are now promoting loans against securities collateral, while Merrill Lynch has a cash management and credit card service for customers similar to that provided by commercial banks. It even makes available checks that can be written against a customer's cash balance and will make loans against the equity in one's home.

Merrill Lynch has broadened the spectrum of finance-related services it offers. In its move to establish a nationwide real estate brokerage network, it has acquired a mortgage insurance firm, a mortgage life insurance company, a real estate financing firm, and an employee relocation business.

The United States stock exchanges, an important link for the whole investment banking process, could undergo a radical transformation as computers become widely used in trading markets. During the 1980s, regional stock exchanges will become part of an electronically linked National Market System. Such a system should enable all investors, regardless of their location, to buy and sell securities at the best prices available anywhere in the country. This electronic hookup would permit interaction among customers' orders without necessitating intervention by a dealer. Investors would be provided not only with a wider choice of prices on a larger number of stocks but with faster action on orders. Although the National Market System was mandated by Congress in 1975, full-scale implementation lies in the future. Brokers, who would sometimes be bypassed in electronic trading, have resisted such computerization. This has slowed the establishment of a national exchange.

Other changes in the stock exchange are forthcoming. The current auction market system, with stocks traded on an exchange floor, may evolve into a system resembling the dealer market that now exists in bond trading and in *over-the-counter* (*OTC*) stocks, where securities are traded off the trading floor. The new system could develop into a hybrid of the dealer and auction market, where only trades are handled off the board. Stock specialists will survive, but will be a rare specimen. The stock certificate will become extinct as a growing number of transactions are recorded in computer memory.

Security markets are often classified into four divisions: exchanges, over-the-counter, third, and fourth markets. Third and fourth markets are sizable, newer markets which are expected to play an increasingly important role in the future. The third market developed in response to the absence of volume commission-rate discounts on the NYSE. The main participants in the third market are institutions such as bank trust accounts, pension funds, insurance companies, mutual funds, and a few select private individuals. These customers reduce their brokerage costs and obtain better prices on exchange-listed securities which they buy and sell at negotiated commissions in the third market (part of the over-the-counter market). Since the third-market makers deal almost exclusively with broker-dealers and institutions, the services offered are minimal.[5] In some cases, a major institutional investor might agree to generate a fixed amount of negotiable-rate commissions for receipt of all research services of a brokerage firm.

The fourth market refers to those institutions and wealthy individuals who buy and sell securities directly among themselves, completely bypassing the broker. The market is essentially a communications network among block traders. The fourth-market organizer may collect a small commission or a flat annual retainer for helping to arrange these large transactions. The fourth market represents a competitive force in the marketplace and encourages the exchanges and the OTC to handle large blocks efficiently at a lower cost. Several privately owned fourth-market organizations facilitate this type of transaction.[6]

The small investor might suffer if these changes take place, as he will not enjoy the same access to inside markets available to institutions. Consequently, he may seek ways to invest through mutual funds or other types of institutional vehicles which are large enough to have leverage into the inside market. Mutual funds will represent a popular way for the small investor to tap the equity market. Small investors in the year 2000 are likely to be older, better educated, wealthier in terms of assets and income, and better informed. At the same time, they will have the luxury of expanded communication channels, with more investor affairs conducted over the telephone. They may even have access to a cathode ray tube where they can observe transaction data, as well as a printer for presenting hard copy for tax records. Bills could be paid from home via terminals or phone on a routine basis as EFTS become more acceptable to customers.

Attracting the higher net-worth individual in order to sell a broad array of retail services may well be the basic strategy of most retail banks and retail-oriented brokerage firms. They will offer the widest range of retail services, including all kinds of money management services and trust and estate programs that today are available only to a few. In fact, consumer banking will embrace total financial management and planning. The consumer will be able to choose between highly automated services at lower prices and highly personalized services at higher prices.

Knowledgeable consumers will probably continue to view each financial need as a separate activity and seek the most advantageous product or service in each financial area. Firms seeking to develop one-stop financial services for the public may find not only that they have to overcome the retail customer's natural resistance to change in dealing with a broad range of financial companies but also that this consumer selectivity suggests that Merrill Lynch's CMA may be used primarily for its convenient access to an account offering a high rate of return on excess funds and liquidity and not for its credit card and margin borrowing features.

What is the future of the investment banking industry? One particular concern of the securities industry is the competitive advantage that major commercial banks would have in selling financial services by leveraging off of their commercial lending powers. If brokerage firm managements conclude that mergers with banks will be precluded in the foreseeable future, they might reason that it would be futile to wait for a buyout offer from a bank and that they might as well sell out now to another type of institution. Alternatively, some managements would see no need for a merger at all in the absence of competition from the banking industry, especially if their company's finances, strategy, and competitive position are sound.

The Chase Manhattan Bank has established a new subsidiary for its investment banking activities that will be capitalized at $175 million. Chase has merged its domestic and international securities trading and capital market activities into a single subsidiary of the bank. Chase will be engaging in underwriting government, quasi-government, and general obligation bonds of states and municipalities. It will also be involved in private placements, the arrangement of mergers and acquisitions, and corporate financial advisory services. Chase would also like to underwrite corporate and revenue bonds, which is not permitted by the Glass-Steagall Act.

Advest, a regional brokerage firm based in Hartford, was seriously considering the purchase of a savings and loan association now that they have enhanced powers to offer money market funds and to offer limited commercial loans. Inter-Regional Financial Group Inc.—which owns Dain Bosworth Inc., in Minneapolis, Rauscher Pierce Refsnes Inc., in Dallas, and operates a total of 71 brokerage outlets in 20 states— has announced that it plans to open its first savings and loan association some time during 1983 in Minneapolis. It also may add a thrift institution in each of its markets. Inter-Regional's move into the savings and loan field is part of a strategy to diversify its earnings base to reduce dependence on the securities business. Deregulation and lower interest rates have improved the profitability of the thrift business. This is particularly true in the case of a new savings and loan association, which is not burdened by a portfolio of low-rate mortgages.

It looks as if competition in the investment banking and brokerage businesses is going to be intense. Larger capital bases may be required if these firms are going to be able to survive. If the cross-selling opportunities presented by the mergers of some brokerage firms into insurance companies and other financial conglomerates appear to work, additional mergers may take place in the years ahead. The competition from the broker-bankers, the bank-owned discount brokers, the financial conglomerates, the role of shelf registrations, and the possible emergence of savings and loan associations in the retail securities distribution function will challenge the creativity of independent firms in the fight for survival.

NOTES

1 Martin R. Blyn, "The Evolution of the U.S. Money and Capital Markets and Financial Intermediaries," in M. E. Polakoff and T. A. Durkin, *Financial Institutions and Markets*, 2d ed., Houghton Mifflin Company, New York, 1981, pp. 35–36.

2 Ibid., p. 34.

3 S. L. Hayes III, "The Transformation of Investment Banking," *Harvard Business Review,* January–February 1979, p. 53.

4 H. D. Shapiro, "Shakeout in the Discount Game," *Institutional Investor,* December 1981, pp. 146–151.

5 J. C. Francis, *Investments: Analysis and Management,* 3rd ed., McGraw-Hill Book Company, 1980, pp. 52–54.

6 Ibid.

CHAPTER
EIGHT

The concept of the *mutual fund* found its roots over 140 years ago in Europe when William I established in Belgium the "Société Générale des Pays-Bas pour favoriser l'industrie nationale." However, the

MUTUAL FUNDS

real pioneer in the field, the Foreign and Colonial Government Trust, was formed in London in 1868. The purpose was to provide "the investor of moderate means the same advantages as the large capitalists, in diminishing the risk of investing in Foreign and Colonial Government Stocks, by spreading the investment over a number of different stocks."[1]

With the growth of the American economy in the late nineteenth century and the beginning of the twentieth century, many types of financial institutions appeared on the scene to provide a means of investment. As early as 1823, a New England life insurance company had features that resembled those of an investment company. Investment companies were established toward the close of the nineteenth century by bankers, brokers, and investment counselors in Boston, New York, Philadelphia, and other cities who saw the need of making diversification and professional financial management available to investors of moderate means.[2]

Following the Great Depression and failure of some financial and industrial organizations, the SEC launched a study of investment companies which culminated in the Investment Company Act of 1940. This act was designed to provide the statutory safeguards for the investor, providing a framework within which the mutual fund industry has grown substantially. Mutual funds are now the fourth largest type of financial institution in the United States.

There are two basic types of mutual funds—*open-end* and *closed-end.* Unlike ordinary mutual funds, which sell unlimited shares that can always be redeemed at their net asset value, closed-end funds have only a set number of shares outstanding that are generally traded on the major exchanges. They often sell at large discounts from their net asset value. A number of closed-end funds have become open-ended in the last few years and brought handsome profits to investors who had purchased them at a discount.

The traditional mutual fund industry, which consisted of stock and bond funds, began in the 1940s and peaked in assets at $57 billion in 1972.

In 1970, close to 90 percent of the mutual fund sales involved *load products*—products for which a sales charge is added on top of net asset value of the fund. By 1980, however, 98 percent of sales were on a no-load basis. The no-load mutual fund industry now represents a major asset category where there is limited salesperson contact.

Another salient development in the mutual fund industry has been product line proliferation. In the last decade, fund complexes have introduced what we call a "family of funds" with a wide variety of investor needs being satisfied. The mutual fund industry introduced tax-exempt funds, international funds, option funds, long-term corpo-

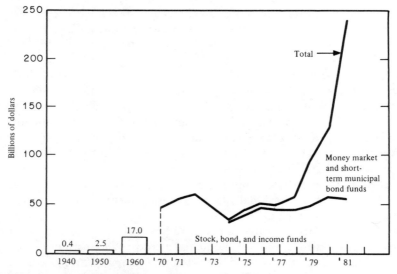

FIGURE 8-1 Growth of mutual fund assets, 1940–1981. (*Source: Mutual Fund Fact Book, 1982.*)

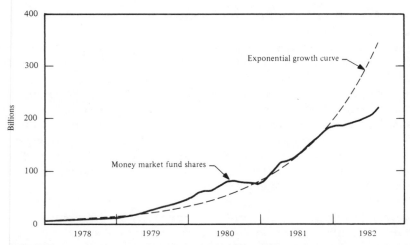

FIGURE 8-2 Growth of money fund assets, 1978–1982. (*Source: Goldman Sachs Economics, September 1982.*)

rate bonds, intermediate-term bonds, short-term bonds, junk bonds, high-yield bonds, and highly popular money market funds.

Changes in the regulatory environment, inflation rate, investment preferences, and attitudes of the brokerage community have significantly changed the mutual fund industry in the last decade. The result is that the industry has come alive again after a discouraging 5 years following the bear market in stocks during the period 1973–74. The mutual fund industry has experienced enormous change germane to image, asset mix, breadth of product line, growth rate, primary method of distribution, types of shareholders, and marketing requirements. By the end of 1981, the mutual fund industry had grown to $250 billion, with almost all of the growth having come from the money fund sector (see Figures 8-1 and 8-2).

At this writing growth is continuing, although the momentum has slowed. The mutual fund industry grew by 70 percent in 1981, the largest asset growth to occur in the industry's history. While the phenomenal popularity of money market funds powered this expansion, by growing from $77 billion in 1980 to $183 billion in 1981 and to $212 billion by mid-year 1982, sales of common stock mutual funds were also strong. The number of shareholder accounts now totals close to 18 million compared with 12 million in 1980.

In less than a decade money market funds have captured the fancy and savings of millions of Americans. Money market funds were the clear winners in the financial revolution until the banks were permitted deregulated accounts. The money funds had pulled deposits away from the nation's thrift institutions and commercial banks because of their higher yields, convenience and liquidity options.

As previously mentioned, the money market funds did have a clear advantage over depository institutions since the funds were exempt from reserve requirements, bank examination processes, deposit restrictions, interest rate ceilings, and other mechanisms which were put in place to safeguard the public against the possibility of another financial crash. The funds themselves are simple in design: they pool money from many consumers and use the funds to buy Treasury bills, commercial paper, certificates of deposit and other short-term investments that earn high money market rates. There are even tax-free money market funds for those in the 50-percent tax bracket.

To many individuals who could not afford to invest $10,000 in a Treasury bill or a 6-month bank certificate, it was the only way to obtain high interest rates available in the money market. For others, who could afford these investments, the funds provided a diversified portfolio of holdings with virtual liquidity. For still others, the funds offered checking accounts that paid interest. Even large companies, pension plan managers, and bank trust departments make use of money market funds. Since a bank trust department may not commingle agency and trust monies in a master note or in an in-house short-term money fund, outside money market funds are utilized. These money funds even maintain separate accounts for each investor. A side benefit of this is that a money fund provides a bank trust department with free accounting services, something not available with a master note arrangement.

Given the phenomenal growth of money market funds so far in the 1980s with their limited capital needs and their ability to generate large profits in a simple spread business, what is then the future outlook for these funds? They do face a number of challenges. It will be a true test for the money market funds to see how well their current products hold up in a period of declining interest rates and in a fully competitive environment now that interest rate restrictions on depository institutions have been removed. Banks and thrift institutions will have one important advantage in that they will offer the consumer insurance on deposits of up to $100,000. However, money market funds may wish to offer a variety of alternative investments to compete with bank insurance coverage:

1 An uninsured fund similar to what is presently available to investors
2 A fund with a private insurance company guarantee, offering a slightly lower yield to investors to help pay for insurance protection
3 A fund that invests only in Treasury bills and notes

A number of mutual funds have already established government funds for more conservative investors. In the light of a growing list of bank and corporate failures, consumers may become frightened and seek investments in high-quality Treasury issues. The list of bank failures in 1982 exceeded 40, including eight savings banks, while the list of corporate failures set a record.

Another potential threat to the money market funds might come from reserve requirements on transaction accounts established by the Federal Reserve. At that point the money funds would probably set up a separate savings account fund with no checking option that would not require reserves and a separate transactions fund account that would enable investors to maintain checking accounts and be subject to reserve requirements.

There still exists a great deal of growth potential for the entire mutual fund industry. Just as there are millions of individuals who have never flown, there are even more consumers who have no money market fund investments and who could be attracted into these funds. There are still a few hundred billion dollars in low-yielding consumer pass-book accounts in depository institutions, as well as quite a bit of money in low-yielding consumer certificates that will be available for potential investment over the next year or two. There is also the business savings account customer who is only earning a passbook type of rate on the maximum $150,000 on which the business is entitled to earn interest in this type of bank account. Other areas of growth should come from sweep arrangements with depository institutions and new funds that will be introduced.

We can expect to see a number of new mutual fund products and services offered to consumers and businesses over the next few years as the competition for funds increases. This increased competition may bring with it a reduction in management fees.

Some funds may attempt to use their distribution system to sell personal insurance product lines. Inexpensive group insurance packages could be advertised via a mass marketing approach such as a "stuffer" included along with the monthly financial statement. Just as some insurance companies have become affiliated with various professional groups or association-sponsored business to sell insurance, money market funds could offer either insurance or their family of money market funds on a similar basis.

At this writing, at least two funds are seriously exploring the possibility of setting up dollar-denominated money market funds abroad, and one fund is considering the establishment of a multicurrency fund for investors in this country. It will be interesting to see if the money market funds, which have so far been the clear winners in the financial revolution, will be able to successfully meet the challenges that lie ahead by developing new products and services. On the other hand, given the high price that Aetna paid for Federated, some of the private investment management and mutual fund companies may choose to sell out to the corporate giants and not go to battle.

On the other hand, Dreyfus has chosen to continue to battle. Dreyfus Corporation, a mutual fund company, has filed an application with the U.S. Comptroller of the Currency to establish its own national bank. The bank would provide trustee, investment management, and administrative services to small and medium-sized corporate pension and individual retirement plans. The bank may eventually offer deposit accounts to its customers and to the general public, but it is not expected to make commercial loans.

This action by Dreyfus occurred one week after President Reagan signed legislation permitting banks and thrift institutions to establish the equivalent of money market fund accounts. Prior to the President's authorization for depository institutions to establish accounts free of interest rate controls, Dreyfus announced plans to buy Lincoln State Bank in East Orange, New Jersey. The Dreyfus application is viewed as a move that further blurs the distinctions among financial institutions.

E. F. Hutton Group had previously set up a trust company to manage select pension and retirement accounts, and Shearson/American Express, Inc., owns a trust company through its Boston Company subsidiary. Other money management companies similar to Dreyfus operate trust companies. The advantage of setting up trust units is that they enable money managers to use pooled funds under trust agreements without registering with the Securities and Exchange Commission.

The change in the law that permits depository institutions to compete directly with money market funds may force money market funds to establish more convenient retail locations (perhaps even ATMs) and to find a way to compete with the depository institutions' ability to insure the money of customers.

Let us now take a look at another giant competitor, the insurance industry, and its competition with the other financial intermediaries for both consumer and corporate funds.

NOTES

1 *Mutual Fund Stock Book,* 1980, p. 10.
2 Ibid., p. 16.

CHAPTER NINE

The concept of *insurance,* or assurance, goes back to ancient times. Babylonian traders "insured" their caravans against loss. They financed them with

INSURANCE

loans that had to be repaid only if the caravans arrived safely. The Greeks applied a similar practice to their seaborne trade. The Romans developed burial clubs to provide funeral funds for members; later, the clubs provided benefits to survivors of the deceased—the rudimentary beginnings of life insurance. The first insurance company, in what is now the United States, was established in Charleston, South Carolina, in 1735. Fire insurance companies were established in New York in 1787 and in Philadelphia a few years later.

Let us look at the structure and statistical makeup of this important industry:

1 In the United States today, just under 2 million people are employed in the insurance industry (see Table 9-1).
2 The industry consists of just under 5000 companies (see Table 9-2) and is one of the largest members of the financial services sector, as well as one of the most important investors in the U.S. money and capital markets.
3 The insurance industry can be categorized by product line (life, property and casualty, health) or by ownership (mutual versus stock). The leading life insurers are Prudential, Metropolitan, Equitable, Aetna, John Hancock and New York Life, while the largest of the property and casualty insurers include State Farm, Allstate, Aetna, CIGNA, and Travelers (see Table 9-3).

TABLE 9-1
EMPLOYMENT IN THE INSURANCE INDUSTRY, 1978–1981
(ANNUAL AVERAGES)

	PROPERTY AND CASUALTY COMPANIES	OTHER COMPANIES	AGENTS, BROKERS AND SERVICE PERSONNEL	ALL INDUSTRY
1978	446,900	726,700	592,600	1,766,200
1979	467,600	732,200	625,100	1,824,900
1980	477,100	747,000	652,300	1,876,400
1981	475,900	756,900	665,600	1,898,400

SOURCE: Company data, Bureau of Labor Statistics, U.S Department of Labor; agents, brokers, and service personnel and all-industry figures. Bureau of Labor Statistics data adjusted to account for American Council of Life Insurance estimates of additional independent agents and staff personnel.

TABLE 9-2
BREAKDOWN OF U.S. INSURANCE COMPANIES BY TYPE, 1981

	PROPERTY AND CASUALTY INSURERS	LIFE INSURERS
Stock	1542	136
Mutuals and others	1452	1842
Total	2994	1978
Grand total	4972 insurance companies	

SOURCE: American Council of Life Insurance

TABLE 9-3
LEADING PROPERTY AND LIFE INSURANCE COMPANIES BY REVENUES, YEAR-END 1981 IN BILLIONS OF DOLLARS

LEADING PROPERTY INSURERS PREMIUMS WRITTEN*		LEADING LIFE INSURERS LIFE INSURANCE IN FORCE	
1. State Farm	8.5	1. Prudential	456
2. Allstate	5.4	2. Metropolitan	394
3. Aetna Life & Casualty	4.0	3. Equitable	224
4. Travelers	3.0	4. Aetna Life & Casualty	164
5. INA	3.0	5. John Hancock	146
6. Hartford Fire	2.9	6. New York Life	137
7. Continental Insurance	2.7	7. Occidental Life	124
8. Liberty Mutual	2.7	8. Travelers	116
9. Farmers Insurance	2.7	9. Connecticut General	91
10. Fireman's Fund	2.5	10. Lincoln National	73

* Excludes life and health premiums.
SOURCE: company annual reports.

TABLE 9-4

LEADING STOCK AND MUTUAL INSURANCE COMPANIES BY ASSETS, YEAR-END 1981, IN BILLIONS OF DOLLARS

LEADING STOCK COMPANIES IN TERMS OF ASSETS		LEADING MUTUALS IN TERMS OF ASSETS	
1. Aetna Life & Casualty	39.6	1. Prudential	71.6
2. Travelers	21.6	2. Metropolitan	51.8
3. Connecticut General*	18.0	3. Equitable	36.8
4. Hartford Group	11.7	4. New York Life	21.0
5. Allstate	11.5	5. John Hancock	19.9
6. INA*	11.0	6. State Farm	18.9
7. Lincoln National	9.0	7. North Western Mutual	12.2
8. CNA	8.9	8. TIAA†	11.4
9. American General	8.1	9. Massachusetts Mutual	9.1
10. Continental	8.1	10. Bankers Life Of Iowa	8.8

* Merged in 1982 to form CIGNA with $28.7 billion in assets.
† TIAA, a nonprofit stock company, functions as a mutual.
SOURCE: company annual reports.

4 The six largest mutuals ranked by assets are Prudential, Metropolitan, Equitable, New York Life, John Hancock, and State Farm, while the six largest stock companies are Aetna, CIGNA, Travelers, the Hartford Group, Allstate, and Lincoln National (see Table 9-4).

5 The $4 trillion in life insurance in force (see Table 9-5) generates annual premiums (life, annuity and health) in excess of $107 billion (see Table 9-6).

6 The total net premiums written by property and liability companies for all lines, including accident and health, are close to $100 billion annually (see Table 9-7) while total assets approximated $228 billion in 1981 (see Table 9-8).

7 Although *ordinary life insurance* still outranks group insurance, *group insurance* appears to be growing more rapidly. Term or decreasing *term insurance* accounted for over 43 percent of ordinary life insurance purchases in 1980 compared to 20 percent in 1970, while most group insurance purchased was term insurance. Females accounted for 22 percent of life insurance purchased in 1980 compared to 12 percent in 1970. These trends should continue during the 1980s.

8 Automobile insurance is still the dominant property and casualty line, accounting for close to 41 percent of all written premiums, while *workers' compensation* accounts for just under 15 percent of net written premiums. Other large lines include liability other than auto (8.0 percent), homeowners multiple peril (10.0 percent), commercial multiperil (7.0 percent), and fire and allied lines (5.0 percent).

TABLE 9-5
LIFE INSURANCE IN FORCE IN THE UNITED STATES, 1900–1981, IN MILLIONS

YEAR	ORDINARY NO.	ORDINARY AMT.	GROUP CERT.	GROUP AMT.	INDUSTRIAL NO.	INDUSTRIAL AMT.	CREDIT NO.†	CREDIT AMT.	TOTAL NO.	TOTAL AMT.
1900	3	$ 6,124	—	—	11	$ 1,449	—	—	14	$ 7,573
1905	5	9,585	—	—	17	2,278	—	—	22	11,863
1910	6	11,783	—	—	23	3,125	—	—	29	14,908
1915	9	16,650	*	$ 100	32	4,279	—	—	41	21,029
1920	16	32,018	2	1,570	48	6,948	*	$ 4	66	40,540
1925	23	52,892	3	4,247	71	12,318	*	18	97	69,475
1930	32	78,576	6	9,801	86	17,963	*	73	124	106,413
1935	33	70,684	6	10,208	81	17,471	1	101	121	98,464
1936	33	72,361	7	11,291	83	18,863	1	138	124	102,653
1937	34	74,836	7	12,638	85	20,104	1	216	127	107,794
1938	35	75,772	7	12,503	85	20,396	2	256	129	108,927
1939	36	77,121	8	13,641	85	20,500	2	307	131	111,569
1940	37	79,346	9	14,938	85	20,866	3	380	134	115,530
1941	39	82,525	10	17,359	87	21,825	3	469	139	122,178
1942	41	85,139	11	19,316	90	22,911	2	355	144	127,721
1943	43	89,596	13	22,413	94	24,874	2	275	152	137,158
1944	46	95,085	13	23,922	98	26,474	2	290	159	145,771
1945	48	101,550	12	22,172	101	27,675	2	365	163	151,762
1946	53	112,818	13	27,206	104	29,313	3	729	173	170,066
1947	56	122,393	16	32,026	106	30,406	5	1,210	183	186,035
1948	58	131,158	16	37,068	106	31,253	6	1,729	186	201,208
1949	61	138,862	17	40,207	107	32,087	8	2,516	193	213,672
1950	64	149,116	19	47,793	109	33,415	11	3,844	202	234,168
1951	67	159,109	21	54,398	109	34,870	12	4,763	209	253,140
1952	70	170,875	24	62,913	111	36,448	14	6,355	219	276,591
1953	73	185,007	26	72,913	112	37,781	18	8,558	229	304,259

Year										
1954	76	198,599	29	86,410	111	38,664	21	10,046	237	333,719
1955	80	216,812	32	101,345	112	39,682	28	14,493	252	372,332
1956	83	238,348	35	117,399	110	40,109	32	16,774	260	412,630
1957	87	264,949	37	133,905	108	40,139	34	19,366	266	458,359
1958	89	288,607	39	144,772	104	39,646	35	20,536	267	493,561
1959	93	317,158	41	160,163	102	39,809	38	24,998	274	542,128
1960	95	341,881	44	175,903	100	39,563	43	29,101	282	586,448
1961	97	366,141	46	192,794	98	39,451	45	31,107	286	629,493
1962	99	391,048	49	209,950	95	39,638	47	35,341	290	675,977
1963	102	420,808	51	229,477	93	39,672	52	40,666	298	730,623
1964	104	457,868	55	253,620	92	39,833	58	46,487	309	797,808
1965	107	499,638	61	308,078	89	39,818	63	53,020	320	900,554
1966	109	541,022	65	345,945	88	39,663	69	58,059	331	984,689
1967	113	584,570	69	394,501	84	39,215	70	61,535	336	1,079,821
1968	116	633,392	73	442,778	81	38,827	75	68,357	345	1,183,354
1969	118	682,453	76	488,864	79	38,614	78	74,598	351	1,284,529
1970	120	734,730	80	551,357	77	38,644	78	77,392	355	1,402,123
1971	123	792,318	82	589,883	76	39,202	76	81,931	357	1,503,334
1972	126	853,911	85	640,689	76	39,975	78	93,410	365	1,627,985
1973	128	928,192	88	708,322	75	40,632	78	101,154	369	1,778,300
1974	131	1,009,038	94	827,018	71	39,441	84	109,623	380	1,985,120
1975	134	1,083,421	96	904,695	70	39,423	80	112,032	380	2,139,571
1976	137	1,177,672	100	1,002,647	67	39,175	78	123,569	382	2,343,063
1977	139	1,289,321	106	1,115,047	66	39,045	79	139,402	390	2,582,815
1978	142	1,425,095	111	1,243,994	64	38,080	84	163,081	401	2,870,250
1979	146	1,585,878	115	1,419,418	62	37,794	84	179,250	407	3,222,340
1980	148	1,760,474	118	1,579,355	58	35,994	78	165,215	402	3,541,038
1981	149	1,978,080	123	1,888,612	55	34,547	73	162,356	400	4,063,595

Note: "Credit" is limited to life insurance on loans of 10 years' or less duration. "Ordinary" and "Group" include credit life insurance on loans of more than 10 years' duration. Totals for "In the United States" represent all life insurance (net of reinsurance) on residents of the United States, whether issued by U.S. or foreign companies. Beginning with 1959, the data include Alaska and Hawaii.

* Fewer than 500,000.   † Includes group credit certificates

SOURCE: *Spectator Year Book* and *American Council of Life Insurance.*

TABLE 9-6
PREMIUM RECEIPTS OF U.S. LIFE INSURANCE COMPANIES, 1977–1981, IN MILLIONS OF DOLLARS

	1977	1978	1979	1980	1981
LIFE INSURANCE PREMIUMS					
Ordinary	$24,161	$26,341	$27,970	$29,463	$ 35,331
Group	6,855	7,285	8,007	8,508	8,997
Industrial	1,299	1,280	1,320	1,323	1,474
Credit	1,450	1,686	1,786	1,535	1,554
Total Life Insurance Premiums	33,765	36,592	39,083	40,829	47,356
ANNUITY CONSIDERATIONS					
Individual	4,552	4,454	4,976	6,504	10,384
Group	10,422	11,885	12,963	17,526	18,198
Total Annuity Considerations	14,974	16,339	17,939	24,030	28,582
HEALTH INSURANCE PREMIUMS					
Individual	5,009	5,505	6,081	6,366	6,531
Group	17,741	19,382	20,838	22,262	24,437
Credit	830	942	975	738	835
Total Health Insurance Premiums	23,580	25,829	27,894	29,366	31,803
Total Premium Receipts	$72,319	$78,760	$84,916	$94,225	$107,741

Note: Credit life insurance is limited to insurance on loans of 10 years' or less duration.
SOURCE: American Council of Life Insurance.

TABLE 9-7
TOTAL NET PREMIUMS WRITTEN BY PROPERTY AND LIABILITY INSURANCE COMPANIES, 1956–1981, IN THOUSANDS OF DOLLARS

	ACCIDENT AND HEALTH	ALL OTHER	TOTAL		ACCIDENT AND HEALTH	ALL OTHER	TOTAL
1955	$ 915,624	$10,214,448	$11,130,072	1976	$2,120,152	$58,693,166	$60,813,319
1960	1,357,800	13,515,031	14,972,631	1977	2,315,734	70,080,195	72,396,929
1965	1,643,848	18,419,820	20,063,468	1978	2,827,884	79,082,047	81,689,931
1970	1,903,841	30,953,185	32,857,025	1979	3,179,250	85,943,389	90,122,519
1975	1,920,412	48,146,153	49,966,565	1980	3,290,764	92,233,735	95,579,549
				1981	3,585,113	95,690,462	99,275,575

SOURCE: Best's *Aggregates & Averages.*

TABLE 9-8
ASSETS OF U.S. INSURANCE COMPANIES, 1981, IN MILLIONS OF DOLLARS

	PROPERTY AND CASUALTY INSURERS	LIFE INSURERS
Stock	166,693	221,487
Mutuals and others	61,536	304,316
Total	228,229	525,803
Grand total (Year end 1981)	754,032	

SOURCE: American Council of Life Insurance

IMPACT OF THE FINANCIAL REVOLUTION ON THE LIFE INSURANCE INDUSTRY

Let us start our discussion of current trends by looking at the life insurance industry. First and foremost, the life insurance business has shifted away from the sale of whole life and endowment policies as an investment vehicle toward term and group insurance. There has also been a structural shift toward the "living concept" or longevity emphasis and toward such products as annuities, tax shelters, guaranteed return vehicles, financial planning, and administration of funds. The life insurance industry continues to suffer from highly competitive pricing (declines of more than 50 percent in premiums per $1000 of insurance coverage), policy loans, policy cancellations, and increased expenses. For example, outstanding policy loans exceed $40 billion out of the approximately $150 billion of cash value that could conceivably be borrowed. With the price of new insurance products falling rapidly, older policies on the books are becoming increasingly vulnerable to replacement. This has given numerous aggressive companies and agents a much larger market to go after since it includes the older policy base of more mature companies. In fact, it appears that the loss of older policies has accelerated rapidly during the past year and is becoming a meaningful problem to more mature companies with traditional whole-life bases. It is clearly an indication that the existing base of older policies is not immune from a life insurance price war. Though large, cash-rich companies can weather such a price war for a long period, the higher degree of competition is likely to continue to stimulate further consolidation within the life industry. Thus, increased economies of scale in companies with older policy bases have become more of a necessity in order to control rising costs and servicing expenses.

Underwriting profits in life companies have been pressured not only by price competition but also by rapidly rising costs related to inflation. Of course, the problem has not been without some attempt at solution. Those companies which have converted to automated accounting and collection of premiums and have integrated data and word processing into their organizations have, in most cases, improved home office, policy processing, and service costs. In addition, certain distribution modes besides the traditional agency system have achieved lower, more efficient distribution of insurance to lower and middle class buyers. Examples are mass marketing, group and cluster sales, specialty product emphasis, association selling, and brokerage systems.

On the plus side, mortality experience for the life industry has been positive over the past decade. The death rate per 1000 has fallen from 7.1 in 1970 to 6.1 in 1978. In addition, the average life span for the total population has increased three years from 70.2 to 73.3 between 1968 and 1978. With major advances in genetic research and cancer treatment and with the decreasing mobility of the population resulting in fewer auto fatalities, the average life span could improve further. Overall, these trends should help the entire industry's profitability on older policies that remain in place.

However, serious problems exist within the distribution or marketing systems of most insurance companies. As a result, there has been a tendency to shift toward mass marketing and group sales as a better way of controlling distribution and marketing expenses. Furthermore, it is highly likely that we will see less use of agents in the future and more use of mass marketing via home computer–telephone–cable TV hookups that will enable financial products, services, and transfers to be sold through the home electronics media. This would cut distribution costs considerably and allow price-sensitive consumers even better product prices for insurance. Note that direct marketing through mail, credit cards, and other media make particular sense for smaller life policies and special coverages such as health, disability, and travel accident insurance. Selling by mail is another way to reduce distribution costs. Estimates indicate that mail order sales of all categories of insurance exceeded $4 billion in 1981. Direct marketing is expected to become a growing method of selling insurance and the most efficient way of achieving better market penetration. Another sales method—

the selling of insurance through financial institutions—also offers the advantage of lower costs because premiums could be added to the mortgage credit card payment.

HEALTH INSURANCE   Now, let us take a look at the health insurance industry. Health insurance has been written in the United States since before the Civil War, when it began by providing protection against loss of income related to accidents and certain diseases. Modern health insurance started in the 1930s with the beginning of associations similar to Blue Cross. More than 9 out of 10 persons have some form of private health insurance coverage, a remarkable increase from the ratio of 5 out of 10 in 1950. Since the 1930s, life insurance companies have become increasingly important in providing health insurance as a form of prepayment for, and protection against, hospital and medical costs. New forms of protection, particularly major medical expense plans, long-term disability coverage, and dental insurance have grown rapidly.[1]

During the past decade, group health insurance has emerged as a growth business, especially for the multiline insurance organizations. Although the companies had difficulty in the late 1960s in adjusting to Medicare, the group health business has become profitable because it has become a business of fees rather than underwriting risk. Note that the concept of fee income as a successful business for the financial services revolution is a recurring theme in this book. Most large group business is written on an experience-related or cost-plus basis. Consequently, except for some inevitable year-to-year volatility, premium and profit growth have outpaced inflation. Above-average growth in medical care expenditures and increasingly comprehensive coverage have increased premiums.

The Reagan Administration is now attempting to introduce competition into medical care and delivery systems and encourage private enterprise, thereby hoping to lower inflation in medical costs. One possible effect of the Administration's efforts is that the shifting of costs from the public to the private sector could cause a surge in costs for insurers, and the inevitable lag in premium rate adjustments could cause a temporary profit squeeze. However, in a few years, the new competition in medical care may reduce the rate of increase in medical costs about the time that the premium increases, which could boost profits.[2]

CONSOLIDATION IN THE
INSURANCE INDUSTRY

Within the last 15 years, the insurance industry as a whole has experienced a number of mergers and acquisitions by large conglomerates and holding companies, among them ITT, American Express, Continental Group, American Brands, and Connecticut General/INA. Industrial companies have been major purchasers of life insurance companies, because earnings stability, lower tax rates, and expectation of receiving dividends from a corporate subsidiary at an 85 percent tax-free rate have proved attractive. This evolution toward larger companies is expected to continue, consequently reducing the number of independent insurance companies.

John Cox, chairman of the INA Insurance Group, in a keynote speech to the 1981 Financial Analysts Federation Insurance Seminar, began his remarks by noting that the insurance industry is currently undergoing change at a faster rate than at any time in its history. He sees two types of companies evolving from this transition period:

1 Large multinational asset protectors
2 Efficient marketers of financial services

Companies in the first category will act as huge asset collectors which will provide product diversity on a global basis. There will be relatively few companies of this type because of the numerous consolidations taking place among present insurers. These firms will have access to a vast worldwide underwriting capacity for insuring the enormous asset values of such commercial risks as oil tankers and rigs, refineries, and nuclear power plants.

The second group will experience economies of scale resulting in lower premiums, while specialization will ensure greater expertise for the services provided. Consequently, this group should experience more rapid growth. Because there will be little product differentiation, the most efficient insurers, who have the most technologically efficient systems and the lowest overhead, will make the most money.

Cox also predicted that eventually every person and every commercial venture will buy just one policy to protect against any conceivable loss. He also forecast that the number of worldwide insurance distributors will be reduced to maybe 50 or 100 carriers because insurance companies are basically inefficient, spending almost 40 cents on the dollar between either distribution or administration of the underwriting and claims.[3]

Cox also stated that "Access to the computer and the blossoming of the managerial sciences have given the industry unparalleled ability to instantaneously manipulate information . . . It will allow us to develop standardized contracts within easy reach of the cost-conscious consumer. It will allow the individual buyer to comparison shop, and it will make for increased efficiencies and increased professionalism in our distribution system."[4]

INSURANCE IN A CHANGING
ENVIRONMENT Cox is most likely right about the future of the insurance industry, but there is even more involved in the structural changes than he points out. Indeed, the future development of the insurance industry will be shaped by social, technological, financial, and regulatory influences. The socioeconomic transition now underway in the United States, as well as in the mature industrial societies of Europe, is characterized by complexity, saturation of traditional growth, rising social costs, and a plateauing of historical trajectories of technological development.

As Roy Anderson, vice president for strategic affairs for Allstate, commented,

> We have broken loose from Western industrial society . . . our institutions are now changing . . . and a new society will emerge, probably within the next couple of decades. It is this concept of changing civilization that explains why some of the problems we have encountered in our systems of insurance seem to defy solution, that is, liability insurance, health insurance, and Social Security. . . . In each of them I see evidence of a systemic breakdown, of the possibility of an impending traumatic change.

Inflation, new lifestyles, the increasing importance of working women, rising incomes, greater longevity, and consumerism have had an impact on some types of older insurance protection and have necessitated new types of insurance. These new offerings clearly reflect today's emerging trends:

- [ ] Homeowner policies have been modified to deal with escalating real estate values, a rise in condominium ownership, and increasing property values and homeowner's warranty packages.
- [ ] Charge account insurance has appeared that will make payments on outstanding bills in case a worker is laid off.
- [ ] Divorce insurance is now available to cover legal expenses.
- [ ] Specialized products for senior citizens, teachers, military officers, and government employees are available.
- [ ] Small business package policies are available.

☐ Extrapolation of the package plan to provide total asset protection needs of the large business client are being developed.
☐ Insurance for investors in mutual funds offers protection against a loss on investment over a specified time frame.
☐ Institutions are providing fringe benefit packages that include many functional insurance needs. Homeowners, personal, auto, and dental insurance may even become part of tomorrow's fringe benefit package.
☐ Insurance policies offer extended warranties on a new car beyond the period covered by the manufacturer.
☐ Insurance protection is available for the valuables in safe deposit boxes.
☐ Broadened insurance for dental treatments, vision care coverage, and legal consultations is being offered increasingly by employers on a group basis or as fringe benefits.
☐ "Inconvenience" policies that pay benefits to an airline passenger whose trip is cancelled by the travel company or who is put in a place other than the intended destination because of a hijacking have become more popular.
☐ Greater competition and lower prices.

Fundamental demographic changes that are transforming the traditional financial security system of the American family will likely shape the life insurance industry as well. Emergent family patterns, shaped by increased divorce as well as by the increase in two-income households, have given rise to a new and different family economic unit. In addition, changing fertility and mortality rates have altered the age structure of the American population.

☐ The school-age group represents a significantly smaller proportion of the population than in earlier decades.
☐ The 65 and over age group has grown substantially and is expected to continue to grow both in number and as a percentage of the total population.
☐ The proportion of the population in the 15 to 39 age group has increased in recent years, and further increases are projected.

Growing concern about the rising costs of Social Security benefits is compounded by this demographic shift. The decreased birth rate evidenced recently and the projected continuation of this low rate will result in an eventual decrease in the number of beneficiaries per 100 covered workers. However, sharp increases in retirees are expected during the next two decades; the number could soar by the year 2010.

These trends in fertility and mortality have several implications:

☐ Higher average retirement ages may be needed to limit transfer payments to the elderly.
☐ Income devoted to the care and education of the young will probably decline.
☐ In the future, major advances in aging research could significantly increase pension and annuity costs with relatively little offset in life insurance costs.

Labor force changes likely to be of primary importance in the development of future life insurance markets include:[5]

☐ The emergence of women as a major source of labor supply beyond traditionally stereotyped female jobs
☐ The emergence of minorities as a significant source of labor supply in major urban locations for other than the lowest level labor jobs
☐ The increase in the average educational level of the labor force
☐ The shift in the age distribution of the work force
☐ The increasing concentration of the work force in large urban, suburban, and semiurban corridors
☐ The growth in the work force and in the number of employees
☐ The unpredictable variations over time in numbers of workers and numbers of jobs available

The increased participation of wives in the work force provides a huge new market for life insurance. However, research has found that agents have sold less insurance to families in which both parents work than to single wage-earner families. Apparently, they view neither the replacement of the husband's income after death nor the replacement of the wife's income as a necessity. Perhaps the second income is considered by couples as a substitute for insurance. Whatever the case, the fact remains that agents are not selling adequately to this high-income group, despite a real need and an ability to buy. Individuals born during the World War II baby boom represent another prime market for life insurance sales.

The demographic, economic, and social conditions described above will continue to determine consumer needs. With the growth of institutionalized security, attitudes toward insurance purchases and estate planning are changing. Current American values and lifestyles foretell of the decreasing importance of leaving an estate to heirs. Concern is shifting from "saving for a rainy day" toward preserving a desirable lifestyle.

People today feel that the best legacy that they can provide their offspring is an education. After that, they will dip into their own estate to provide comforts and pleasures of life. Home ownership has become a highly desired goal. Life, medical, auto, and homeowners' insurance are considered by most individuals to be necessities as long as their costs do not substantially reduce their standard of living.

While some insurers have responded to the changing times by offering new products to fit a changing environment, other insurers have taken defensive measures such as:

☐ Offering higher deductibles and raising premiums, encouraging *self-insurance*
☐ Outright avoidance of writing high-risk insurance
☐ The refusal to underwrite more than a fraction of untried programs, such as the ill-fated government swine flu vaccine program

These trends have prompted broader risk management strategies and the development and growth of captive insurance companies.

Another problem plaguing the insurance industry is the changing social environment which has increased arson, theft, white-collar crime, and fraudulent claims. The changing values of Americans, marked by a shift toward self-gratification and a decreasing respect for the law, has contributed to these developments.

A strong social-mindedness permeating the courts has also resulted in an escalation of court awards in the field of liability—a trend likely to continue all over the world. Unfortunately, despite the fact that it raises insurance costs for everyone, large claims do not appear to be slowing down. Indeed, the mushrooming of tort liability problems, speculative claims, entrepreneurial lawyers, ever more pervasive third-party interpretations of product liability, and medical malpractice have resulted in increased liability claims and increased insurance costs. This "psychology of entitlement" has led to huge awards in disability suits.

Another complicating factor is the sue-if-possible attitude that is currently prevalent in our society. It seems oddest when it crops up among those who freely—and deliberately—take risks such as skiers. The thrill of skiing is provided partly by the possibility of a spill. By the same token, the wilderness camper who beds down in grizzly-bear country is not expecting wall-to-wall safety.

The increased tendency of injured parties to sue somebody has several roots. One is a heightened public awareness that governmental agencies, private companies, and individuals are vulnerable to lawsuits. In addition, the publicity given to big judicial awards awakens greed. Years of activist consumerism have also made people more alert to claims against institutional America. Finally, the act of suing has become less personal. When the defendent is an institution or professional group, people do not suppose anybody is getting hurt until higher insurance rates and higher doctors' bills have a personal impact.

REGULATION OF INSURANCE   Another problem for the insurance industry, as it is for many parts of the financial services industry, is regulation. Senator Thomas Eagleton of Missouri once commented, "There is no longer a question of there being a federal role in the insurance field. That already has been established on the broad front. The only issue remaining is the kind of role it will play."

One thing does seem likely—state regulation will not be superseded or removed. Some states are applying political pressures to hold down personal automobile insurance costs and to change the techniques used by insurance companies to price their product. Many state legislators and regulators feel that auto insurance has become a right and that premium rates should be based on affordability. Private insurers have been coerced into accepting substandard risks and into pricing their service with the result that, in effect, one class of drivers subsidizes another through the insurance medium.

It is unlikely, however, that we will go all the way in regulation. After nearly 30 years of bills and debates on National Health Insurance, little in the way of actual federal programs has actually occurred. Support for federal control or intervention has come primarily from organized labor and senior citizens groups, while opposition continues to come primarily from the medical professions and to some extent from the health insurance industry.

A likely result could be a program which utilizes the current health delivery system while requiring some sort of universal coverage for that small segment of the population not now covered by insurance and providing for catastrophe coverage for individuals. Cost restraint has been a salient element in most proposed bills. The current trends toward deregulation, financial limitations, and lack of desire for new taxation is expected to provide an environment for gradualism and heavy private involvement.

This is small comfort to the insurance industry, which is constantly under attack from consumer groups, state regulators, and the federal government. Consumer complaints about the high cost or unavailability of automobile and homeowners' insurance, as well as charges of discrimination against minorities, have been increasing. In fact, the growth of residual markets, the talk of national health insurance, and growing needs for flood insurance and nuclear pools suggest an expansion of government risk bearing.

The industry is also running into problems because of privacy laws. There are new limitations on access to information on individuals' health, credit, and income—information necessary for a proper assessment of risk. Without access to appropriate data sources, many small insurance companies as well as larger ones will be at a competitive disadvantage in pricing their product. Also, if Public Law 15 (removal of antitrust exemption for insurance companies) is changed, confusion could be created because insurance companies are accustomed to pooling data and operating in a cartel environment for rate making.

B. P. Russell, Crum & Forster's chairman, does not feel that "the federal government has much appetite to take over regulation of the insurance industry," except, he said, "on the issues of availability and affordability of insurance in urban areas." The "redlining issue" is making an impact upon the insurance industry as some states attempt to mandate the availability of homeowners' coverage for some inner city areas.

Government coercion to channel financial resources directly toward the achievement of certain social objectives is a distinct possibility. Also, the inclusion of investment income in rate making could reduce rates to unprofitable levels. This could lead to increased insolvency among insurers.

RESPONSE OF INSURANCE COMPANIES TO THE CHANGING
ENVIRONMENT The rapidly changing environment in which insurance companies must operate has led to structural change within the insurance industry. This change is evident in the development of new classes of risks that require insurance—for example, environmental risk, genetic liability (coverage against genetically transformed microbes escaping from a laboratory), space flights and colonization, drilling platforms, and supertankers.[6] While the advent of new technology promises many market opportunities by the year 2000, the lack of historical loss data and the uncertainties associated with this technology will present the industry with new problems.

As many risks are driven into the exotic or hard-to-place category, consumer pressure and courtroom awards seem to be working to take the flexibility and profitability out of writing certain types of insurance. Political protests that manifest themselves in worldwide terrorism, hijacking, and kidnapping have added to the difficulties of underwriting.

Because of these events, political risk insurance has begun to appeal to a growing list of multinational firms. This insurance protects companies doing business abroad from losses related to nationalization or confiscation of properties, currency embargoes, repudiation of contracts, and cancellation of export and import agreements. While this may boost profits in the near term, the unpredictable risks involved may lead to losses of catastrophic dimensions due to the difficulties in assessing and measuring the degree of risk.

Another trend is increased competition. The property and casualty industry, in particular, can expect more intense competition among existing companies and from mutual life companies, foreign-based insurers, and captives (firms owned or controlled by another concern and operated for its needs rather than for an open market). This competition will also carry over into the *reinsurance* field as the direct insurers become more active in insuring risks of other insurers. Increased competition and price cutting will probably always remain a challenging problem and produce an underwriting cycle.

Insurance companies will also become more active as insurance advisors and risk managers in supporting the growth of captives. These captives, as well as being self-insurers, have become profit centers, insuring not only their own companies, but the commercial risks of other companies as well. These captives will become even more active in the reinsurance market.

Another development that adds an element of structural change to the industry is the formation of the New York Insurance Exchange and the Exchange of the Americas in Miami. These new exchanges have syndicates which underwrite risks and transact business in a manner similar to that of Lloyd's of London. The Insurance Exchange operates in a free trade zone and exempts large commercial risks and special classes of unique and unusual coverage from New York State Insurance Department rate and policy form regulations. This "New York Lloyd's" could impose a serious threat to the American business of Lloyd's of London once it amasses enough capacity and underwriting experience.[7]

Ralph Saul, Chairman of CIGNA, in the keynote address at the World Insurance Congress in Philadelphia, described a marketplace where insurers will provide risk management services on a fee basis rather than accept risk themselves for an uncertain reward. He also commented that ATMs and two-way cable television systems are forging electronic links among banks, brokers, and insurers in a process of convergence that "could change totally the way financial services are delivered to individuals. . . . There appears to be little need for direct selling of personal lines."[8]

A significant key to the trends in the insurance industry will be what happens to Lloyd's, the most famous insurance company in the world. The future of London's insurance market is important because a shift away from London's supremacy would represent a significant transformation of the world's insurance business. However, Lloyd's has problems even now. The development of new insurance lines, the penetration of international markets by both American and European insurers, fluctuations in the international currency market, and the growing significance of reinsurance present great competitive challenges to British insurers.

Indeed, several direct challenges to Lloyd's have already been made, threatening London's position for the future:[9]

☐ The New York Insurance Exchange, a reinsurance market modeled after Lloyd's, could eventually pose a serious threat to the large volume of American business currently placed at Lloyd's of London (American business currently accounts for half of Lloyd's business).

☐ The establishment of the New York exchange indicates a capacity for innovation among American insurance companies and brokers. Even if the exchange fails, the new American reinsurance companies which have become prominent during the past 5 years will begin to undermine Lloyd's powerful hold on the American market as the excess demand for reinsurance gives way to an excess supply.

☐ Other threats to Lloyd's brokers are the takeover of a leading Lloyd's broker, Leslie and Godwin, by Frank B. Hall and the indication by Marsh and MacLennan that it too would like to acquire a London broker.

☐ With the thrust of many of the American insurance companies into the international market, Lloyd's will face greater competition.

While American brokers at Lloyd's should benefit the British position in that they will add to the flow of insurance from the United States, British brokers could respond by merging with American brokers in order to secure American business directly. If Anglo-American brokers become a reality, the American insurance market will open to even more international competition.

Still another trend in the industry is the pursuit of new international markets. As competition and increasingly unfavorable regulatory environments threaten American and European markets, insurers are beginning to generate business in the developing countries of the Third World. In Africa, Asia, and Latin America, a number of rapidly growing countries are extremely underinsured. Their great potential lies in consumer insurance and life assurance as well as in liability lines. In Asia and Latin America, insurance premiums increased 15 percent annually between 1965 and 1980. These developing countries have no choice but to bring in foreign insurers—or more often, reinsurers—to provide large portions of their insurance needs.

Developing countries must seek foreign insurance for several reasons:

☐ Lack of capital
☐ Lack of insurance expertise
☐ Excessive concentration of risks in their cities and in large insurance plants
☐ The unbalanced nature of their insurance needs resulting from the relative lack of small consumer risks

The cost of insurance for all developing countries has resulted in the introduction of measures by some developing countries to restrict the outflow of insurance business. Restrictions in foreign ownership mean little, however, if the government fails to control reinsurance.

REINSURANCE   In an attempt to block the penetration by foreign reinsurers, many countries have established state-owned reinsurance companies. As they grow larger and develop their underwriting skills, many national reinsurers are likely to begin operating in a manner similar to ordinary commercial reinsurers in developed countries. Reinsurance companies from the Third World are emerging as a major force in reinsurance. These companies, which have a great need to spread their risks, will almost certainly contribute to the world's reinsurance overcapacity as they become larger and more aggressive marketers.

The increasing emergence of catastrophe risks, in which a single exposure unit can have an enormous loss potential, is likely to bring about fundamental changes in insurance companies' approaches to risk. Traditionally, variation from expected losses has been reduced through the underwriting of a large number of risks and through reinsurance. Reinsurance and insurance pools have been used to cover those risks that have catastrophic loss potentials.

The types and enormity of technological advances will present greater, but less clearly defined, risks. Such risks have been handled through arrangements utilizing nuclear pools, marine pools, and Lloyd's of London. The future rise of such arrangements is projected to increase in direct proportion to the increasing number and size of claims involving catastrophic loss, particularly as large-scale energy technologies are implemented. Widespread use of such advanced technologies will increase the volume of both the special risk and the reinsurance business.[10]

A related development is the formation and capitalization of reinsurance companies by life insurers. As maximum probable losses of various risks grow, it can be expected that more life companies will either directly reinsure property and liability lines or establish reinsurance subsidiaries. The Prudential Reinsurance Company is representative of this trend. Also, it can be expected that there may be some mergers among mutual life companies to help cut costs and other overhead expenses.

THE INSURANCE AGENT Another problem facing insurance companies, as we described earlier, is the high distribution cost of insurance. Indeed, it seems certain that there will eventually be a thinning of the ranks of agents because of substantial change in technology used by companies in both generating new business and improving record keeping and computerized information systems. It is also expected that there will be a change in the way in which agents are compensated. New-business commissions are expected to be higher than commissions on renewal business, while agent compensation will be more closely linked to underwriting results.

It is highly probable that the independent agent will eventually be bypassed. The agent will be replaced by a branch bank, stock brokerage, or consumer finance distribution system or by a computer–television–telephone hookup in the home.

One of the problems facing the agency system is the difficulty of coping with the continuous erosion of the market share to direct writers and life insurers. As costs go up, the independent agent's business will get tougher. Price competition will necessitate streamlining the distribution system and will force out inefficient operations. Agents are likely to continue to have the greatest difficulty in coping with present and future pressures of the insurance business for several reasons:[11]

☐ The carriers have continued to exert efforts to cut commissions.
☐ Volume requirements by carriers retard the entrance of new agencies into the business.
☐ Direct writers have obtained significant portions of the personal lines business previously written by independent agents. There are indications that direct writers, as well as life insurance companies, will continue to move more into commercial lines.

The role of the insurance *broker* has also begun to change. Brokers are broadening the services they offer and the control they maintain over their own organizations. In addition to acting in their normal capacity with insurance companies, brokers have begun to offer risk management consulting services to business clients. They have helped their clients set up captive insurers and have begun to provide insurance capacity. Merger and acquisition activity is likely to increase as large brokers, as well as foreign and financial firms, seek smaller profitable agencies. Reduced margins, the threat of government intervention, and the presence of new competitors are also placing pressures upon the broker-agency segment of the business.

Commission cuts in personal lines markets and the subsequent wave of agency terminations have resulted in much agent dissatisfaction with insurance companies. While many agents perceive their roles as independent dealers, some dissident factions believe that unionization would provide the primary means by which in-house agency disputes could be resolved.

Private agents and brokers may seek new means to maintain their competitive stance. Smaller houses might have to merge with other local houses in order to meet volume requirements of the carriers. Another possibility would be a combination with a noninsurance organization, such as a financial institution, serving to add monetary strength and new commercial leads.

ACQUISITIONS AND MERGERS Another trend is the emergence of non-insurance company competitors. A look at the following evidence shows that noninsurance firms have shown an increasing interest in the acquisition of insurance agencies and brokerage firms.[12]

☐ Earnings of these companies in the last 5 years have been exceptionally good
☐ As insurance costs have soared, many large corporations have considered the acquisition of an insurance brokerage firm as an effective cost-cutting device
☐ An in-house insurance capability yields advantages not available through the standard client-broker relationship
☐ Lower tax rates in life insurance companies, the stable growth in earnings and the ability to upstream dividends to the industrial company at an 85 percent tax-free rate are all appealing
☐ The potential for "financial gamesmanship" is also appealing to potential industrial purchasers

The growing interest in life insurance company ownership by nonlife companies will continue to influence the industry throughout the decade of the eighties. While the mutual life companies have been entering the property and casulty business, many property and casualty companies (as well as other multinational corporations and conglomerates) have been actively pursuing purchases of life insurance companies. These acquisitions have taken place because of:

☐ Acquisition prospects that are partially insulated from economic and technological uncertainties
☐ Superior performance of many life companies, especially when compared to industrial companies
☐ Favorable current returns and future prospects

However, we do not believe that ownership of agencies by industrial companies is likely to be a major trend in the future. To be sure, organizations such as Esmark and Comerco have sold their agencies. A more likely candidate for involvement in the insurance business is the investment community. Brokerage houses, in addition to realizing good returns on investment, provide potential vehicles for the entrance of large financial corporations into the insurance industry. Stockbrokers believe that they complement insurance brokers. Both are in personal service businesses, providing not only an interchange of clientele but synergies stemming from preexisting organizational structures and services. Investment bankers are also expanding into the life insurance field. Merrill Lynch, Dean Witter, and E. F. Hutton, for example, have acquired life insurance companies, while Dean Witter itself has been acquired by Sears, which owns Allstate.

We have seen insurance companies being acquired by noninsurance firms, brokerage firms being acquired by insurance companies, and life insurance companies being acquired by brokerage firms. Now let us look at the recent mergers and acquisitions of a number of the largest companies in the insurance industry.

While the Prudential-Bache and American Express–Shearson mergers appear to focus on selling new financial and insurance products to individuals at retail, the Connecticut General-INA union (CIGNA) is aimed at corporate customers. It represents the long-range strategy of seeking to sell group insurance coverage to individuals through their employers. The combination of INA's products in health, automobile, and property coverage with Connecticut General's establishment position in corporate employee benefit plans offers much promise. Group coverage for auto, home, and health insurance sold to individuals through employee benefit programs will have lower premiums and lower operating costs. INA's international arm should help expand Connecticut General's presence in the multinational corporate arena. This acquisition involves more than the typical buying-for-value concept, as both of these companies were looking for ways to diversify their assets and marketing ability and to avoid an unfriendly takeover by a noninsurer.

Aetna Life & Casualty Company, the nation's largest stockholder-owned insurance company, has been moving rapidly into the financial services market and into nonfinancial fields. The company acquired an 86 percent interest in Federated Investors, Inc., an investment company with $27 billion under management. Federated is mainly a manager of money market funds that it oversees for bank trust departments. It also provides banks with discount stock-brokerage service and "sweep" facilities which allow banks to automatically invest checking account balances above a certain level in money market funds. In addition, Aetna has purchased a 40 percent interest in Samuel Montagu, a British merchant bank. The Federated and Montagu transactions show Aetna's desire to carve out a niche in providing financial services to corporations and financial institutions in the United States and abroad. The Aetna approach is different from the approach used by some rival insurance companies which have bought securities firms with big retail networks that serve individuals.

To fill a gap in its financial services, Metropolitan Life Insurance Company agreed to acquire State Street Research and Management Company, a Boston-based institutional investment manager with assets of $9 billion under management. State Street, which established the first mutual fund in the United States in 1924, manages funds for major corporations, foundations, and endowments as well as mutual funds.

Another important development is the entry of large life insurance companies into the property and casualty industry, which occurred over the last 10 years and which will eventually have a great impact within the industry as these companies improve market share and underwriting results. Although the startup costs (including adverse loss experience) have been substantial, the larger mutual life insurers have entered the property and casualty industry for a variety of reasons, including:[13]

□ Greater retention of agents
□ One-stop selling (property and casualty business should open doors and lead to greater opportunities for life-health sales)
□ Long-range profit
□ Diversification

□ Defensive measures (given the hazy future of health insurance and whole life insurance)
□ Utilization of enormous financial capacity

It is clear that large life companies will continue to grow in the property and casualty business, especially in the personal lines. Their profitability should ultimately be equal to those companies that are well established. It should be noted, however, that a number of insurance experts expect the management of some life insurance mutuals to panic when they have abominable underwriting results during the next property and casualty cyclical downturn. This could lead to the withdrawal of some of the mutuals from offering property and casualty insurance.

MASS MERCHANDISING   One likely trend, which we have already touched on briefly, is the increased use of mass merchandising— e.g., mail solicitation, television and radio commercials, and group- or association-sponsored business—to reduce underwriting costs by eliminating the need for an agent. Another benefit is that if automatic payroll deductions or arrangements to have the firm's premiums collected through VISA and MasterCard are allowed, the likelihood that customers would let their policy lapse would be reduced.

A first sign of the coming trend was Prudential's bid to win the group health insurance contracts of the National Retired Teachers Association (NRTA) and the American Association of Retired Persons (AARP). The bid was made in order to develop its direct mail operations. These contracts would generate a level of premium volume large enough to justify developing such a capability.

In addition, the rapidly growing senior citizen market is sizable; 52 million people will be over the age of 55 in the year 2000. Prudential has excellent potential for further market penetration within NRTA and AARP because only 17 percent of the combined membership purchases the group health coverage sponsored by the two organizations. Also, Prudential was able to enter into the NRTA and AARP relationships without alienating its present agency force since this business had always been marketed on a mass merchandising basis.

Mass merchandising techniques will be utilized to sell individual retirement accounts. There will be great competition among insurance companies, banks, mutual funds and investment companies on television and radio, in newspapers and magazines, and in mailings to individuals. The potential to capture a major new source of funds under management is great as the changes in tax laws make it advantageous for every working American to set aside $2000 per year from 1982 until retirement. These funds will not be taxed until withdrawn upon retirement and should lead to a higher savings rate in the United States.

DEVELOPMENTS IN ELECTRONIC
DATA PROCESSING
New technology is having a major impact on the insurance industry. Property and casualty underwriters have built large data bases which form the core of their management information systems. These information systems enabled companies to increase the productivity of workers and reduce expense ratios during the seventies. Insurers have made the computer easily accessible to employees in home and branch offices, as well as in independent agencies, where they have automated at least some clerical and accounting functions. During the eighties, the most significant application of *electronic data processing* (EDP) communications technology will be an industrywide interface network between independent agents and their carriers. Agents will be able to enter pertinent underwriting information into their microcomputers and send these data directly to those insurers for premium quotations. After an insurance company is selected, the policy will be issued from the agent's microcomputer. Insurers will also extensively utilize satellite data transmission and teleconferences. Both technological advances will save enormous amounts of time and money.

Irwin Sitkin of Aetna Life and Casualty, speaking at the Financial Analysts Insurance Seminar in New York in June 1981, forecast that by 1990 Aetna's office functions would be automated through the use of text processing systems, which should substantially increase the productivity of the company's office employees. A primary item on Aetna's list of EDP communications projects is the development of a distributed data processing network for agency-company interfacing. At least 25 percent of Aetna's 8800 agents should be hooked up to this network by 1985. Sitkin predicted that by the end of the eighties the technologically advanced insurance companies will be able to complete insurance transactions in an applicant's home via a personal computer hooked up to cable TV.

WHAT ARE SOME OF THE FAST
GROWTH AREAS OF THE
INSURANCE INDUSTRY?
For an industry not typically known for innovation, life insurers have done wonders in the pension business

since 1974. At the end of 1977, over 19 million people were covered by pension plans with United States life insurers. The array of new product offerings has been staggering, varying from equity real estate separate accounts to accounts that vary with the Consumer Price Index. The basic offerings of the industry revolve around two factors: contracts guaranted by principal and interest rate returns for a given number of years of service.

Over the past decade, the life insurance industry's most rapid growth area has not been life insurance at all but what could be considered the reverse of life insurance—annuities. The annuity concept is hardly new, but it was a virtually unnoticed part of insurance industry operations until 1974. That year marked the enactment of the Employee Retirement Income Security Act (ERISA), which resulted in sharply increased demand for actuarial and administrative services. In the wake of the 1974 stock market debacle, ERISA also helped to usher in guarantees on pension returns in the form of fixed-income portfolios. The emphasis on good portfolios—performance combined with aggressive marketing efforts—has resulted in huge gains in pension fund management by insurance companies.

Another new form of insurance that has gained a lot of popularity is universal life. It is far more flexible than most other insurance products in that payments are made into a savings fund that yields a tax-deferred interest rate. Enough money is withdrawn from the fund to pay life insurance premiums. Essentially, the policy tries to purchase term insurance with tax-sheltered annuities. However, most annuities have a fixed interest rate, whereas the yield changes periodically with market conditions. The universal policy has the added advantage of flexibility regarding the frequency and amount of payments made by the investor. This policy also has the benefit of flexibility that enables the investor to add extra money to the savings fund or increase insurance coverage. Funds can also be withdrawn or premium payments made from cash value benefits.

However universal life is not an insurance policy for everyone. While this product and other flexible life insurance products are likely to be instigators of much replacement activity, they will not completely replace whole life insurance. With the advent of variable-rate mortgages and consumer loans, the fixed-rate installment payment method of providing for future financial security will still hold appeal for a portion of the population. The universal life product appears to be an opportunity for the industry to recapture lost savings dollars.

So far we have concentrated on the revenue, or cost, side of the insurance industry. However, another important aspect is the huge investment portfolios of insurance companies.

INVESTMENT PORTFOLIO
PHILOSOPHY

Insurance companies are broadening their perspective on investment portfolio philosophy. They have shown greater interest in what might be classified as "nonconventional" investments or tangible assets rather than the traditional portfolio of publicly held stocks and bonds (see Table 9-9). Negative real interest rates in the late 1970s encouraged investments in rapidly appreciating tangible assets such as oil and real estate. Investments in commercial satellites, energy exploration and development, leveraged leasing, commercial real estate, and a plethora of private placements, including commercial lending to corporate clients, have heightened the shift in philosophy. The volatility of equity market prices and the high yields offered within the traditional bond market have led to a relative decline in common stock assets held by both life and property or casualty insurers.

Within the last year many life insurance companies have returned to more traditional investments in paper assets. Weakness in the prices of real assets, plus historically high real interest rates have led to the shift back toward investments in money market instruments and bonds.

Life insurance companies also began to increase their residential mortgage holdings in 1978, following a 10-year period of reduced holdings. There was also a keener interest in commercial real estate investments and mortgages. However, in recent years, Metropolitan Life,

TABLE 9-9
INVESTMENT MIX OF TOTAL ADMITTED ASSETS BY
U.S. LIFE INSURERS IN 1981

	VALUE, IN HUNDREDS OF THOUSANDS	PERCENTAGE OF TOTAL
Government securities	$ 39,502	7.5
Corporate bonds	193,806	36.9
Common stock	35,408	6.7
Preferred stock	12,262	2.3
Mortgages	137,747	26.2
Real estate	18,278	3.5
Policy loans	48,706	9.3
Cash	4,279	.8
All other	35,815	6.8
Total admitted assets	$525,803	100.0

SOURCE: A. M. Best.

TABLE 9-10
PERCENTAGES OF CHANGING DISTRIBUTION OF INVESTMENT ASSETS
OF U.S. LIFE INSURERS, 1940–1981

| YEAR | GOVERNMENT SECURITIES | CORPORATE | | MORTGAGES | REAL ESTATE | POLICY LOANS | MISCELLANEOUS ASSETS |
		BONDS	STOCKS				
1940	27.5	28.1	2.0	19.4	6.7	10.0	6.3
1950	25.2	36.3	3.3	25.1	2.2	3.8	4.1
1960	9.9	39.1	4.2	34.9	3.1	4.4	4.4
1970	5.3	35.3	7.4	35.9	3.0	7.8	5.3
1980	6.9	37.5	9.9	27.4	3.1	8.6	6.6
1981	7.5	36.8	9.1	26.2	3.5	9.3	7.6

SOURCE: American Council of Life Insurance.

which has about $15 billion invested in commercial real estate, has been quietly slowing its commitment of funds to real estate development. The company believes that the offices, hotels, and shopping centers now under construction will cause an oversupply of rental space in many market areas. The excess supply will worsen as the aggressive building of commercial property in recent years coincides with the damage that the economic downtown of 1981–82 may do to the ability of many prospective tenants to pay the high rents dictated by the high cost of financing new construction.

The life insurance industry is faced with a number of potential problems related to its investment portfolio. Policy loans have become a serious problem with many companies who specialize in whole life insurance since borrowing rates against the available cash value yield only between 5 and 8 percent for life insurance companies. Fully invested companies are often forced to sell bonds at a loss, to increase their borrowings in the commercial paper market, or to draw down their credit lines at commercial banks at rates in excess of the yield on policy loans in order to meet the demand for these loans from policyholders. The companies also have large portfolios of low-yielding bonds which might yield only 75 percent of book value if immediate liquidation were required. The potential for lower total returns on real estate investments is also entirely possible as the investment public appears to be shifting toward financial rather than tangible assets. The changing distribution of investment assets of life insurance companies can be seen in Table 9-10.

The cyclicality of the underwriting cycle in the property and liability insurance industry (see Figure 9-1) leads to a different type of investment portfolio for property and casualty companies than for that of life insurance companies. The holdings of mortgages for property insurers represent under 1 percent of investment portfolio holdings compared to close to 27 percent for life companies. The holdings of their corporate bonds are also well under 10 percent of assets, compared to close to 37 percent for the life industry. On the other hand, common stock holdings are close to 20 percent of total portfolio holdings compared to under 10 percent for the life insurers. Tax-exempt holdings of bonds are close to 39 percent for property and casualty companies, while they are practically nonexistent in life company portfolios. While policy loans accounted for 9 percent of life insurance company investments in 1981, property and casualty insurance companies have no such problem. Their greatest problem is the huge volume of underwriting losses suffered in 1979, 1980, 1981, and 1982, in addition to heavy losses in their fixed-rate bond portfolios. These underwriting losses

Underwriting Gains and Losses after Policyholder Dividends
Property and Casualty Insurance Business 1956-1981 (In Billions of Dollars)

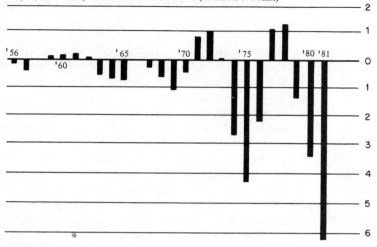

Investment Income, Property and Casualty Insurers*
1956-1981 (In Billions of Dollars)

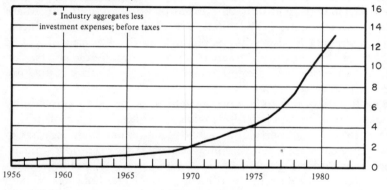

Combined Net Income* before Taxes, Property and Casualty Insurers
1956-1981 (In Billions of Dollars)

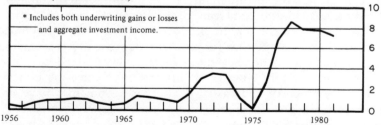

FIGURE 9-1 Underwriting cycle of property and casualty insurers. (*Source: Insurance Information Institute, based on data from Best's Aggregates & Averages. Reprinted in Insurance Facts, 1981-1982.*)

TABLE 9-11
PERCENTAGES OF CHANGING INVESTMENT MIX OF U.S. PROPERTY AND CASUALTY INSURERS, 1970–1981

	INVESTMENTS OF PROPERTY/ CASUALTY INSURERS			
	IN 1981	IN 1980	IN 1975	IN 1970
Bonds	74.82	73.72	69.05	62.79
U.S. government	11.73	11.06	10.34	10.30
Other government	0.81	.87	.51	.74
State, municipal, etc.	14.90	14.75	18.10	17.52
Special revenue, etc.	33.23	33.73	24.87	17.43
Railroad	0.31	.31	.37	.63
Utility	3.59	3.50	4.53	5.75
Miscellaneous	9.84	9.06	9.78	9.93
Parent, subs., affiliates	0.41	.44	.55	.49
Common stock	18.67	20.13	26.32	33.28
Railroad	.15	.13	.04	.15
Utility	1.52	1.61	2.03	3.97
Bank	.95	.91	1.17	2.34
Savings & loan	—	—	—	.03
Insurance	.86	.78	.26	.43
Miscellaneous	10.53	12.08	10.92	17.17
Parent, subs., affiliates	4.66	4.63	11.90	9.20
Preferred stock	4.96	4.96	3.95	3.37
Railroad	.06	.05	.03	.03
Utility	3.33	3.43	3.14	2.01
Bank	.11	.11	.02	.02
Insurance	.03	.03	.01	.02
Miscellaneous	1.36	1.29	.65	1.17
Parent, sub., affiliates	.07	.05	.10	.11
Other	1.55	1.19	.67	.55
Mortgages	.77	.60	.28	.49
Collateral loans	.09	.06	.06	.05
Other invested assets	.69	.53	.33	—

SOURCE: Compiled by Insurance Information Institute based on data published in Best's *Aggregates & Averages.*

have caused a shift out of tax-exempt bonds into higher yielding tax-ables. It has also restricted the cash flow available for investment pur-poses which, given the historic size of such funds, is a major develop-ment for the capital markets.

The portfolio composition of property and casualty insurance compa-nies can be seen in Table 9-11.

NOTES

1 G. A. Bishop, *Capital Formation through Life Insurance,* Richard D. Irwin, Inc., Homewood, Illinois, 1976, pp. 49–50.

2 Ibid., pp. 51–58.

3 B. Densmore, "The Philadelphia Story," *Business Insurance,* May 26, 1982, p. 1.

4 K. J. McIntyre, "Future Holds Many Challenges for Insurance: Cox," *Business Insurance,* May 26, 1982, p. 4.

5 P. W. Plumley, "Demographics and the Life Insurance Industry," *Best's Review,* May 1978.

6 B. Berlinner, "Development of the Insurance Industry in the Years to Come," *Reinsurance,* December 2, 1977, pp. 20–21.

7 Ibid.

8 B. Densmore, "Insurance Alternatives Changing Market," *Business Insurance,* May 10, 1982.

9 "A U.S. Lloyd's and a Free Trade Zone," *Reinsurance,* vol. 10, no. 3, July 1978, pp. 130–139.

10 "Growing Influence of Reinsurance," *Review,* December 3, 1977.

11 M. S. Lepenfeld, "Insurance Agents and Brokers, A Look into the Future," *CPCU Annals,* December 1977.

12 A. R. Freedman, "Behind the Life Acquisition Boom," *Best's Review,* March 1978, pp. 63–65.

13 W. G. Howland, "Life Insurance Companies in the Property-Casualty Business," *United States Banker,* January 1979.

IMPLICATIONS OF THE FINANCIAL SERVICES REVOLUTION

Before we discuss a suggested course of action for financial institutions, individuals, and investors in the financial revolution, let us briefly recap the salient trends of this revolution. The following list of items summarizes the key elements:

1 The financial services industry is much more competitive now and will continue to be so for the indefinite future. All the institutions in the industry are now offering many new products and services.
2 With barriers to regulation dwindling, the industry is going to undergo some fundamental changes during this decade. The ultimate form will be molded not only by the economic and regulatory environments, but by a changing demographic structure and a new emerging international order. The groundwork has been laid for institutions and holding companies to offer a full range of financial services ranging from commercial and investment banking to insurance and investments.

The now distinct thrift institutions, commercial banks, investment banks, and insurance companies may emerge within a single, integrated holding company encompassing all financial services. The financial services industry will most likely be less fragmented in the future with a trend toward larger firms. Smaller institutions are merging since they have found it difficult to compete against some of the powerful corporate giants and because the takeover offers have been generous. With the relaxation of restrictive regulation these institutions could take advantage of synergies arising from an overlap of marketing systems and from similarities among the services they offer as well as among customer bases.

It is difficult to differentiate between thrift institutions and commercial banks when it comes to servicing the banking needs of retail customers. The blurring of the distinctions among the functions of most American financial intermediaries is beginning to take place. In fact, as financial institutions grow in both size and scope over the next 10 years, it may be difficult to distinguish between Sears, Citicorp, American Express, Bank of America, Merrill Lynch, Prudential, and CIGNA. The near-banks, such as Sears, American Express, Prudential, and Merrill Lynch will play a key role in the future of the consumer financial marketplace.

3 Financial institutions, especially banks, will diversify even further, as they offer more homogeneous, depersonalized products and seek larger market shares. Still many small institutions will be able to carve out a niche in the financial marketplace by offering personal or specialized services or innovative products, or by developing more sophisticated marketing and operational skills and consorting with money market funds, brokerage firms, strict research shops selling advice for a fee, options specialists, reinsurance, franchising, networking, estate planning, selling of investment management and data processing services to asset management accounts of money market funds, and mutual fund or pension fund management. The response to the increased pace of change in this case has been the antithesis of diversification—a stripped down, unbundled financial service or product. Thus, one could characterize the new structure of financial institutions as extreme opposites—the establishment of specialized financial boutiques and the establishment of giant multipurpose financial department and variety stores. Of course, some institutions attempt to combine both of these features and offer most financial services while being recognized as specializing in just one or two.

The use of the bank holding company umbrella is enabling commercial banks to evolve toward the European concept of the universal bank and the concept of the variety store or supermarket. Banks have become involved in leasing, various forms of insurance, data processing, financial and economic consulting, and investment banking activity such as merger and acquisition consultation, private placements, offers of commingled trust funds to the public and the underwriting of tax-free general obligation bonds.

Other examples of diversification are large brokerage firms which have begun to offer money market funds to customers, as well as insurance and real estate. Also, some thrift institutions have adopted commercial bank functions such as NOW accounts, commercial savings accounts and loans, a variety of higher-yielding consumer certificates, and real estate management. Insurance companies have added money market funds, annuity packages, brokerage firms, increased term lending to business, real estate, property management, and private placements to their collection of financial services. In summary, diversification and asset acquisition have been the reaction of many large firms toward the changing financial risks and needs of businesses and consumers as the concept of one-stop shopping and financial conglomerates have become a reality.

4 Newly emerging linkages among providers of financial services will be a major force in linking services, geographic areas, and markets. These networks will provide the tie-ins with technology in a complete delivery system. Networking can occur via nationwide linkages of automated teller machines or through the franchising of the products and services of large money center banks. Other examples of networks are the agreements which have been reached between banks, thrifts, brokers, and money market fund administrators. Still another example is the provision of trust services by commercial banks, insurance companies, or investment management companies to thrift institutions, which have recently been granted trust powers but lacked internal expertise.

5 It is likely that there will be a changing structure among financial institutions. Thrift institutions are not likely to evolve into "one-stop" family financial centers or supermarkets for consumers. Instead, thrifts will probably offer more specialized real estate services that include short-term construction, development, and acquisition loans. Indeed, savings and loan associations will probably emulate mortgage bankers and focus on the buying, selling, and servicing of mortgages instead of originating mortgages for addition to portfolios.

6 Consortia of large regional banks may be established to compete with large money center banks who will be seeking out-of-state consumer business, directly or indirectly. These consortia will also

compete against the money center banks for domestic and international wholesale customers. Also, with the increasing diversity and sophistication of services demanded, interstate mergers may be the one way in which banking institutions can achieve the corporate form and capital base needed to compete effectively in the delivery of technologically advanced electronic services.

7 The rapid development of technology is making obsolete the geographic restrictions of the McFadden Act. The holding company umbrella has also enabled companies to offer a broad spectrum of financial services nationwide. There is a good chance that geographic restrictions to bank branching will fade and that we will have nationwide banking within the next few years.

8 Product differentiation may be difficult to achieve. Banking institutions may lose some cost-of-funds advantage over nondepository institutions when Regulation Q is removed. With banks paying even more for consumer deposits, banks will be lobbying to lift the usury ceilings at the state level associated with consumer loans and mortgage loans so that they can participate profitably in this market.

9 The thrift problems are far from solved, and may grow more acute. The issuance of promissory notes by the FSLIC (via U.S. Treasury IOUs) in exchange for income capital certificates by the thrifts represents a bailout attempt to rescue the nation's troubled thrift institutions. However, this legislation does not really solve the problems of the industry because it does not improve earnings or cash flow. The legislation benefits only a limited group: the employees, executives, and shareholders of the thrifts; general creditors; subordinated debt holders; and holders of accounts over $100,000. This seems to be another makeshift approach to dealing with the potential failure of a plethora of thrift institutions. If interest rates stay high or move higher, the net result of this promissory note plan will be nationalization of close to one-half of the industry. These savings and loan associations might be operated much like the U.S. Postal Service.

The apparent congressional attitude is that since government regulation helped create the thrift problem, it is only fitting that the government attempt to offer a solution. However, unless the thrifts are granted full banking powers or immediately select a profitable, specialized niche, they are unlikely to survive unless interest rates are reduced substantially for a sustained period of time.

The rationale that the thrifts must be saved because of their role in financing the housing market is not really true today, although it once may have been. Most thrift institutions which have consumer certificates with deposit maturities of 6 months, 91 days, 18 months, and 30 months are not lending their funds at fixed rates in the long-term mortgage market. They do not wish to run the risk of funding short and lending long in a volatile interest rate market. Clearly then, the thrifts are among the major losers in the financial revolution.

10 The clear winners of the financial revolution are the conglomerates who are able to offer most products and services without any restrictions on geographical location of offices and branches. However, to really gain a dominant foothold in the consumer financial marketplace, these institutions are going to have to develop the ability to cross-sell their products and services. Commercial banks may also emerge as winners as the holding company umbrella permits them to engage in most financial activities, with the exception of life, property, and liability insurance. Although there are restrictions on branch locations for retail deposits, there are no restrictions on the lending side of the balance sheet as banks can make corporate loans anywhere they choose and consumer loans in states outside the one in which they are domiciled if they have a finance company office. Furthermore, with the new sweep arrangements and the lifting of the interest rate ceilings on depository accounts, banks are now competitive with money market funds. They even offer depository insurance on these funds which is not available from most money market funds. However, there is one caveat to nationwide banking: It is questionable whether consumer banking is really a profitable activity since today consumers are essentially paid market rates for deposits and since starting up or operating branches is very expensive.

11 A move toward conglomeration by financial intermediaries should probably continue. The wisdom of this move can be explained from both a defensive and an offensive posture. There has been a need to undertake defensive mergers to protect asset bases in an era of deregulation and to diversify from unstable forms of cash flow across traditional lines of industrial demarcation. There has also been a desire to diversify asset maturities and to cross-market products and services to higher-income families. The setting of a minimum asset is really required to justify taking advantage of deposit generation and asset commitment opportunities as well as of the new electronic networks that could possibly revolutionize the way in which financial services are delivered.

12 "Deintermediation" will increase. Thus, it is entirely conceivable that in the future, banks will make as much or more money on the "flow" of assets through their books as they will from the

assets *on* their books. The first signs of this can be seen in mortgage pass-throughs.

The insurance industry is also moving toward the concept of a fee for service and consultation. Insurance companies are acting as risk management advisors and counselors to corporate clients in helping them to establish insurance captives. The flow-through concept should lead to more fee services as banks and insurance companies reduce credit risk or liability.

13 We will also see greater use of the futures market to offset interest rate risks as banks attempt to better hedge their asset and liability management positions.

14 The growth of a family of money market funds has provided a strong source of earnings for investment companies, brokerage firms, and insurance companies. Money market funds were clear winners in the financial revolution until depository institutions were permitted to offer money market accounts whereupon the lead was largely reduced. Other sources of income for investment banking firms—in addition to the traditional underwriting, trading, and stock and bond brokerage business—have included merger and acquisition fees, insurance, annuities, lease financing, real estate, options, commodities, mortgage-backed pass-through securities, tax-sheltered limited partnerships in oil and gas, and real estate, as well as a plethora of new consumer products such as the Merrill Lynch CMA, and various credit and debit cards.

15 With the new arrangements between commercial banks and discount brokers, it is likely that discounting will continue to grow in popularity. Indeed, the discount brokerage firms have already taken over close to 10 percent of the retail brokerage business.

16 The recent purchase of major stock brokerage firms by conglomerates and insurance companies may continue. We may also begin to see mergers among mutual life insurance companies. It is also likely that the largest brokerage firms will continue to buy regional brokerage firms. The cross-selling opportunities available from the recent mergers of Sears and Dean Witter, Prudential and Bache, and American Express and Shearson Loeb Rhoades offer new potential for increased business. Eventually, Dean Witter salespeople may sell Allstate insurance to their own customer base, and they may sell stocks, bonds, and insurance to the 26 million active Sears credit card holders, while Allstate salespeople may sell Dean Witter money market funds to *their* own customer base or to Sears credit card holders. The same cross-selling opportunities exist at Bache-Prudential and between Fireman's Fund and Shearson/American Express.

The purchase of stock brokerage firms by some of the major insurers could potentially lead to a change in the distribution and delivery system for insurance sales. Also, it is likely that mass marketing will become an even more important method of selling insurance as the industry attempts to reduce distribution and marketing costs.

17 By the end of the decade the ranks of the nation's independent insurance agents could be pared by at least 50 percent. The survivors might bear little resemblance to today's agents. Tomorrow's agents will have expanded their business to include additional financial services and products besides insurance.

The financial service companies of the future are going to do what is necessary to become the low-cost producers in the industry, utilizing direct selling and captive-agent marketing approaches. As market power becomes more concentrated, the independent agent will most likely become a captive to fewer markets and could eventually be eliminated altogether.

Germane to personal life insurance, the high level of financial sophistication will suggest price vis-à-vis service considerations in the decision to purchase. As individuals conduct more of their financial transactions through the telecommunications media, the service provided by agents will become less important to the consumer.

18 In addition to some of the trends mentioned above, the Monetary Control Act of 1980 and the potential for financial deregulation should eventually lead to:

- [ ] A smaller number of surviving financial institutions.
- [ ] High mortgage rates, but a wider selection of mortgage instruments from which to make a selection.
- [ ] The complete elimination of Regulation Q.
- [ ] Cost-plus pricing of loans that will probably lead to higher borrowing costs for corporations and consumers.
- [ ] One-stop banking for select consumers and some corporations.
- [ ] More homogeneous financial services and less market segmentation.
- [ ] Little or no resemblance between tomorrow's banking institutions and many of today's structures in the sense that the high-rent locations and large open spaces may be replaced by more functional, less expensive minibranches and ATM installations.
- [ ] A likely decline in the number of bricks-and-mortar branches. The number of locations at which transactions can be made will increase dramatically as a result of new technologies, the extension of teller machines to workplace and shopping locations, and

the rapid popularization of automatic bill paying, automatic deposit of payroll, and automatic investing.

☐ No separation between the provision of consumer financial services and retailing.

☐ The growth of electronic funds transfers, the interstate mergers of thrift institutions, the national activities of the near-banks, such as Merrill Lynch and Sears, and the recent financial conglomerate mergers acting as a catalyst in promoting interstate banking and the rescinding of the McFadden Act and the Douglas Amendment.

☐ A substantial breakdown of the Glass-Steagall restrictions likely in the next few years with the continuation of merger activity among large financial firms and between financial and non-financial firms. However, this merger activity will no longer be dominated by large nondepository and nonfinancial institutions.

☐ Banking at home via interactive television or computer-television-telephone hookups.

19 Technology will help play a key role in the financial services industry of tomorrow. In addition to debit and credit cards, bill paying and banking by telephone, automated teller machines and point-of-sale terminals, the home computer terminal hooked to both a video screen (television set) and a telephone will accelerate the financial revolution. It is entirely possible that by the year 2000 the way we market goods and services could change dramatically because of the home computer. Competitive price information from the cost of automobiles to the cost of bank loans or insurance may be available on our home computer–TV screen. It is likely that insurance as well as other financial services and products will be available for sale at home. The consumer will have the option to pay for these products and services by using a credit or debit card. This arrangement could potentially lead to a major change in the way we distribute and sell financial products and services as well as other consumer goods. The development of home financial services via new technology may possibly be retarded by cost and consumer concern about the confidentiality of financial information.

As we have suggested throughout the book, the revolution in the financial sector involves major changes for the institutions and employees involved. There are no easy solutions to the problems caused by the convolutions that are revolutionizing the financial services industry, but at this writing, some strategies seem apparent.

RECOMMENDED STRATEGIES FOR
SMALL, INDEPENDENT BANKS

1 These banks are going to face extraordinarily difficult times. The executives and the employees of these institutions must accept this reality and plan accordingly. Many of these banks are inefficient and have high operating costs. Furthermore, they are not adequately capitalized and therefore may not be able to afford the huge capital costs of the new technologies which could eventually reduce costs. It is certain that competitors will have the technology, and thus price competition will intensify.

2 What should these independent banks do? First, the chief executive officers must fully comprehend what is going on. The typical pursuit of traditional, full-service, banking business is probably the wrong approach. Thus, these banks must start to think of themselves and their business in a totally different way. Each bank will have to channel its energies into certain profitable niches. The bank cannot be *all* things to *all* customers. By the same token, the services the bank offers must be looked at from a profit basis, and those services that are not or cannot be profitable should be eliminated. Spread management will probably become the name of the game. Cost controls must be introduced, not just as a temporary phenomenon, but as a permanent fixture. Information systems must be improved to report on costs, assets, loans, spreads, and whatever could affect the bank's profitability. The quality of assets will also be vitally important; in the aftermath of the Penn Square and United American Bank failures, credit quality controls must be tightened up stringently.

3 The board of directors might wish to take the first buyout offer that comes along. At this writing, bigger banks are buying other, smaller, banks with abandon, a practice which may not last for long. It will probably pay to sell out while merger activity is still at its peak and the prices being paid are at reasonable premiums over the current market price of the bank's stock. Small banks run the risk of disappearance and face consolidation just like the thrift industry. The owner or chief executive of a bank can probably negotiate a good employment contract which should give satisfactory job security—at least for a while.

However, if the owners of the bank are unwilling to sell out, there may still be other ways to survive. For instance, the bank could:

1 Become part of a regional consortium of banks, which could then compete with the large money center banks

2 Become a franchisee of a large money center bank
3 Become in effect a local branch of the big bank
4 Close unprofitable branches and concentrate exclusively on profitable locations
5 Buy as many automated teller machines as possible so that the bank can close unnecessary branches and shut down in the evenings and on Saturdays to save on labor and utility costs
6 Develop services and products that can be sold for a fee, and thus generate badly needed cash flow
7 Gain market share by offering fixed-rate loans, making sure, however, to match assets and liabilities and sources and uses of funds as a precaution against unexpected fluctuations in interest rates.
8 Find a profitable niche by offering highly personalized services, extended hours, discount brokerage, income tax preparation, etc.

RECOMMENDED STRATEGIES FOR LARGE BANKS

1 The franchising business with small, independent banks probably makes sense. It will help recover some of the massive front-end costs of technological innovation.
2 By the same token, work on improving the correspondent banking relationships. This, too, will gain a foothold in geographical expansion and could aid in reducing the costs of doing business.
3 Sell data processing capabilities to corporate customers, as well as correspondent banks. In other words, take any excess capacity in data processing capabilities and try to repackage for use at the customer level.
4 Be very selective in acquisitions. Do not waste scarce capital by paying outrageous prices for regional banks. When you do make an acquisition, look for the following characteristics: favorable location and demographics, good earnings record, very limited loan problems, a highly profitable or specialized niche, good distribution system, or superior or unique service offered in local area. Also, be sure the purchase of the bank will allow you to reduce your own costs or increase your profits.
5 With the phaseout of Regulation Q, banks will lose their cost-of-funds advantage. This means that banks will become more and more like pure finance companies. Also, retail banking could become an unprofitable business for the reasons we have discussed earlier.

Therefore, banks will do well to think about getting out of this business entirely unless usury ceilings on consumer loans are raised to allow the bank a profit spread over the cost of deposits.

6 Banks will have to improve their credit quality control and not get caught in the "go-go" growth characteristics in which banks periodically become involved.

7 Banks will have to return to old-fashioned spread management practices where loans are made at a positive spread over the cost of funds with the matching of the maturities of deposits and loans.

8 Banks may wish to use the futures market to lock in their cost of funds in making fixed-rate intermediate-term loans to corporate customers.

RECOMMENDED STRATEGIES FOR THRIFTS

1 Thrift institutions cannot continue to function as they have been. It no longer seems necessary for thrifts to make long-term mortgage loans as that business involves too much risk. In any event, thrifts cannot continue to lend long and borrow short; there must be a matching of the maturities of assets and liabilities.

2 Several options are open to the thrifts. First, they could remain traditional savings and loan institutions. This strategy will only work, however, if their cost of funds declines and the value of the mortgage portfolio rises, which depends on a big drop in interest rates. It is not wise to bet one's survival on an interest rate forecast. A second alternative is to operate as a full-service family bank with a wide range of services, including discount brokerage and insurance. Another opportunity is to operate as a construction lender or a mortgage banking institution. Finally, the thrift could become part of a financial conglomerate including savings and loan, insurance, and brokerage services. The key to which one of these options the thrift chooses is how successfully it performs the particular task.

3 Thrifts can also use the futures market to help them hedge against interest rate risks so that they will be able to make fixed-rate loans to their customers while still being able to lock in a positive spread over their cost of funds.

4 A number of thrifts might combine "lending resources" to compete with commercial banks in making corporate loans.

RECOMMENDED STRATEGIES FOR
INSURANCE COMPANIES
Insurance companies must improve their services in the following ways.

1 Eliminate inefficient distribution systems for personal lines of insurance. They must also lower the cost of commissions without reducing current sales production by insurance agents.
2 Develop improved cost information as a way to keep better control on costs and become more competitive.
3 Purchase a mass marketing distribution company to help in generating revenues and holding down relative costs.
4 Buy or gain access to a home computer and/or cable TV system and sell electronically to a mass market.
5 Expand to other parts of the world where competition is less intense and where profit margins will be larger.
6 Develop sources of fee income and spread business from subsidiaries involved in brokerage, mutual funds, or money market funds.
7 Consider the purchase of an ailing thrift institution if the price is right and assets can be purchased cheaply.
8 Develop an insurance product or policy that will cover the insured against all possible eventualities—one-stop insurance.
9 Get involved in the data processing field, and use this expertise to develop fee income such as tax preparation and management consulting for smaller insurance companies.
10 Consider starting up a new thrift institution that will not be burdened by a low-yielding mortgage portfolio. Recent deregulation and drop in interest rates make this an attractive investment, especially since thrifts can now offer money market accounts.

If insurance companies do not become more efficient, many may fail in the next property-casualty underwriting down cycle. Now is the time to cut costs and develop a strategy for survival.

RECOMMENDED STRATEGIES FOR
RETAIL BROKERAGE FIRMS

1 Competition is reaching a peak among brokerage firms. It is likely that many retail brokers may not be able to survive without a discount securities operation. As mentioned previously, discounters now account for 10 percent of volume. With some discount brokerage

firms now owned by bank holding companies, cross-selling opportunities should lead to growing discount brokerage volume. The retail business is highly profitable for most firms, but that may change under competitive pressures.

2 Brokerage firms must work on developing other sources of income from money market funds, mutual funds, and the existing large customer base.

3 Brokers should learn how to sell life, homeowner's, and auto insurance.

4 Brokerage firms may find it feasible to set up a new savings and loan or buy an existing thrift. They must capitalize on their new powers and insured money market funds.

RECOMMENDED STRATEGIES FOR MONEY MARKET FUNDS

1 Regulatory advantage is fading fast. To survive, money funds must develop technological expertise and a marketing strategy that will attract money from small savers. Also, the money funds' key to survival may be to become the money collection agent for the banking industry.

2 Buy private insurance coverage for money market funds.

3 Funds might consider using their distribution systems to sell insurance and other products.

4 Funds might want to sell out to a financial institution—at the right price—before Regulation Q ends and the fight for survival begins.

5 Money market funds may be at a disadvantage in not having depository insurance, now that banks and thrifts can offer insured money market funds. The purchase of a thrift might be a good competitive move.

RECOMMENDED STRATEGIES FOR EMPLOYEES AT FINANCIAL INSTITUTIONS

1 Do not think that working at a bank, insurance company, or other financial institution is a low-risk, quasi-government job. Although salaries have improved, they may not be commensurate with the risks, particularly in an environment of bankruptcies and mergers.

2 Those who work for a small bank or thrift may do well to look for work elsewhere, even in another industry. The surviving institutions will lay off a lot of people, and even top executives of an acquired company may find themselves out of a job, especially if they earn a high salary.
3 Anyone wishing to stay in the industry should seek employment at the largest and strongest financial institution around.
4 Insurance agents who concentrate exclusively on personal lines insurance may wish to begin to sell commercial lines insurance and other financial products and services to protect themselves against changing distribution systems within the insurance industry.

RECOMMENDED STRATEGIES FOR INVESTMENT AND PERSONAL FINANCE

1 With the apparent trend toward nationwide banking, investors may wish to identify a number of small or even medium-sized regional commercial banks for potential investment. Those institutions with good growth records, a healthy return on assets, specialized niches in attractive locations, and positive demography are candidates for consideration since they may become targets for takeover as the movement toward national banking develops. On the other hand, investors should shy away from bank stocks with large exposure to bad loans.

Investors should also be cautious about purchases of corporate commercial paper and bank certificates of deposit; they must evaluate the credit of the borrower accurately. It is important that people read the prospectus of any money market fund carefully before investing. Credit should be closely analyzed for all investments in corporate stocks and bonds and in municipal bonds as well.
2 With the trend toward electronic banking, home computers, and mass marketing, investors may wish to consider investments in the manufacturers of ATMs, home computers, and cable TV companies. The technological revolution is sweeping the banking industry and creating new growth opportunities for suppliers of automated teller machines. With the appearance of these cash dispensers in bank lobbies, in shopping centers, in gasoline stations, in places of work, and on college campuses, the stocks of ATM manufacturers represent attractive investment opportunities. Along these lines, once the con-

solidation is over, publicly held insurance companies with strong mass marketing programs may also become good investments since they have more efficient distribution systems and are likely takeover candidates.

In addition to the aforementioned cable TV companies and ATM manufacturers, among the beneficiaries of the financial revolution will be those firms involved in advertising and communications. Radio and television networks, magazines and newspapers, the printing industry, and advertising agencies will all benefit from the increased advertising necessary to explain all the different new financial services available to consumers. Advertising agencies that specialize in mass marketing and direct-response advertising (largely labeled in the mind of the public as "junk mail") should benefit substantially as advertisers become more cost- and response-conscious.

3 If investors anticipate a large decline in interest rates, investments in high-quality corporate bonds or even in long-term government bonds could prove profitable. Investors would generate a capital gain as well as a high yield on their investment. Under the declining interest rate scenario, bank liability managers would fund short term in order to take advantage of falling interest rates.

On the other hand, if an increase in interest rates is anticipated, investors should consider selling their bonds and investing their funds in short-term investments. Bank liability managers would usually wish to fund long-term prior to a rise in interest rates in order to minimize the cost of funds to the bank over a specified time frame. Bankers might also wish to sell other fixed-rate assets in their portfolios or hedge against an increase in rates.

4 When money is in short supply, consumers must be cautious of the source they seek. They should be wary, for example, of consolidation loans to pay off numerous outstanding bills. Although it may appear attractive to have a finance company or bank consolidate all debts, it is highly probable that the new interest rate will exceed those rates payable on the smaller loans. If this is the case, it will lead to greater carrying costs. Another potential source of funds is the local credit union. Credit union interest rates for loans are generally lower than comparable bank or finance company rates. Another interesting and sometimes more economical source of borrowing is the stock broker, who can usually loan 50 percent of the market value of stocks and 80 percent of the market value of bonds at a rate that is often just under the prime rate. If difficulty is encountered in meeting mortgage payments, the mortgage lender can help. In most cases the mortgage loan can be rescheduled and payments reduced if necessary. Perhaps the cheapest source of funds at rates

between 5 and 8 percent is to borrow against the cash value of a whole-life insurance policy.

5 Consumers should follow congressional and administrative budgetary actions carefully. If the budget deficit is not reduced substantially over the next few years, we run the risk of interest rates accelerating at extremely high levels, inducing corporate bankruptcies and potentially plunging the economy into yet another recession or stagnation. Supply-side economics can work, but only if we get much lower interest rates.

6 Any increase in bankruptcies among major corporations could severely hurt the operations of the commercial paper market, endanger bank earnings, and have a profound impact on money market funds. Investors could lose confidence in our depository insurance agencies if many more thrifts fail. We might then see a massive flight toward Treasury bills.

There is also the risk that the Federal Reserve may begin to receive intense political pressure to bring interest rates down if corporate bankruptcies continue at recent high levels. This could then bring to a close a reasonably successful battle to abate inflationary pressures in this country. If that is the case, the best course of action would be to avoid long-term fixed-rate bonds and to remain in extremely high quality short-term investments such as Treasury bills.

Thus, conservative investors who wish to minimize risk should invest in government bonds, notes, or Treasury bills. If these minimum $10,000 purchases are made directly from the Federal Reserve, there is no sales charge. Treasury issues can also be purchased through a bank or broker, though a sales fee is charged. Given the risks mentioned above, this may prove a wise strategy. There are also some money market funds that invest almost exclusively in government securities and repurchase agreements.

7 When buying stocks in a fragile economy, the investor must concentrate on lean, strong companies with strong balance sheets, liquidity, and little debt. Firms in growing industries that seem to have costs under control and that seem prepared for a difficult environment should prove to be appropriate investments because unit growth will be important in a period of profit-margin pressure. A disinflation scenario could lead to a shift toward capital spending and away from consumption. Investors might wish to consider firms supplying automated machinery, robots, computers, electronic equipment, and other items that will help industry improve productivity.

8 Consumers should consider using a discount broker for their purchases and sales of stock. They should also consider exchanging their 7.75 and 8 percent 4- to 8-year consumer certificates at deposi-

tory institutions for higher-yielding instruments (despite the interest rate penalty) where the arithmetic makes sense. Also, most consumers should take advantage of the new tax law that enables all working individuals to set aside $2000 per year tax-free in an IRA account. Individuals should also not keep more than $1000 in a passbook savings account because passbook rates pay only a minimal interest rate. Investors should place the amount above $1000 in a money market fund. An investor with at least $2500 can place this money in either an insured money market account or a "Super-Now" account at a depository institution.

9 High-income investors should consider buying tax-free municipal bonds for their portfolios. Tax-free municipal bond funds, tax-free unit investment trusts, tax-free money market funds, and insured municipal bonds should appeal to investors at current high yields. Most investors should purchase new issues rather than issues in the secondary market because of the wide spread between bid and asked prices on already-issued bonds.

GLOSSARY

Acquisition A general term for the taking over of one company by another.

Adjustable life insurance A type of insurance that allows the insured to switch the type of protection, raise or lower the face amount of the policy, increase or decrease the premium, and lengthen or shorten the protection period.

Annuity A contract that guarantees payments that will commence at a specified time and will be payable for a given length of time. It is the actuarial opposite of life insurance: insurance seeks to create an estate, while annuities amortize the estate.

All Savers certificates A tax break under the Economic Recovery Act of 1981 to encourage savings and to help savings and loans cut their costs of obtaining funds by permitting tax-free interest income up to $1000 per individual.

Arbitrage Simultaneous purchasing and selling of the identical item in different markets in order to yield profits.

Automated clearing house (ACH) A computerized facility used by member depository institutions to process payment orders in machine-readable form.

Automated teller machine (ATM) A machine capable of processing a variety of transactions such as accepting deposits, providing withdrawals, transferring funds between accounts, and accepting instructions to pay third parties in a transaction.

Bank credit card A credit card issued by a bank, enabling the borrower to buy goods and services or obtain a cash loan from banks honoring that card.

Bank holding company A company that either owns or controls one or more banks.

Bank Holding Company Act In 1956 the Bank Holding Company Act was passed to restrict the expansion of bank holding companies. It did, however, allow vigorous expansion by one-bank holding companies. In 1970, the Bank Holding Company Act was amended and gave the Federal Reserve the authority under Regulation Y to regulate and control the operations of bank holding companies. Generally, the Federal Reserve has the power to disallow mergers, acquisitions, or other business activities proposed by specific bank holding companies. However, the central bank usually allows bank holding companies to engage in lines of business closely related to banking, provided that such activities will not have an anticompetitive effect.

Banking syndicate A group of banks created for the purpose of underwriting and selling an issue of securities.

Bankwire A private computerized message system administered for and by participating banks through the facilities of Western Union. The system links about 250 banks in about 75 cities. It transfers funds and transmits information concerning loan participations, bond closings, payments for securities, borrowings of federal funds, and balances in corporate accounts.

Bear market A declining securities market.

Bond, municipal revenue Banks now may underwrite a few kinds of revenue bonds, which are obligations backed not by city or state revenues, but by revenue produced by the facilities that are financed; for example, a housing project.

Bought deals The purchase of an entire shelf registration issue by an investment banker for resale (hopefully at a profit) to the public.

Branch banking Any banking system where there are few parent institutions, each having branches operating over a large geographic area.

Broker An intermediary in a secondary market that brings buyers and sellers together; an agent who handles the public's orders to buy and sell securities, commodities, or other property; a sales and service representative who handles insurance for clients, generally selling insurance of various kinds and for several companies.

Broker-dealer A firm that retails mutual fund shares and other securities to the public.

Building and loan association A cooperative or stock society organized for the saving, accumulation, and lending of money.

Call money Currency lent by banks, usually to stock exchange brokers, for which repayment can be demanded at any time.

Cash management account (CMA) An account developed by Merrill Lynch in partnership with Bank One of Columbus, Ohio. Affluent clients are offered a Visa card and a checking account to draw against their investment balances which earn a money market fund interest rate.

Cathode ray tube (CRT) A visual display device that translates the data from a computer memory and visually presents the information in human language form. The CRT enables batches or blocks of information in memory to be instantly accessed, read, and displayed on a screen. In an on-line or real-time data processing system, the device permits instant or impromptu display of any of the stored information.

Cash surrender value The amount available in cash upon voluntary termination of a policy by its owner before it becomes payable by death or maturity.

Central bank The bank that acts as the fiscal agent for the government and as a lender of last resort for financial institutions (primarily banks) suffering liquidity problems. In addition, a central bank (the Federal Reserve in the U.S.) may act to control the monetary base, reserve requirements, and the discount rate and may regulate banking activity.

Certificate of deposit (CD) A negotiable or transferable interest-bearing receipt for funds deposited with a bank, payable to the holder at some specified date in excess of 30 days after issuance.

Clearing House Interbank Payment Systems (CHIPS) An automated clearing facility operated by the New York Clearing House Association which processes international funds transfers among 100 New York financial institutions, mostly major U.S. banks, branches of foreign banks, and Edge Act subsidiaries of out-of-state banks.

Closed-end investment company An investment company, usually specializing in portfolio management of stocks and bonds, that does not offer to redeem its shares and does not sell new shares directly to the public. A fixed number of shares are sold through investment bankers; thereafter, the shares are traded on a stock exchange.

Commercial bank An organization chartered by the state or federal government, the principal functions of which are: (1) to receive demand and time deposits, honor instruments drawn against them, and pay interest on them as permitted by law; (2) to make loans, and invest in securities; (3) to act in a fiduciary capacity.

Commercial paper Unsecured short-term (under 270 days) promissory notes issued by corporations of unquestioned credit standing and sold to corporate and individual investors.

Consortium A grouping of corporations organized to fulfill a combined objective or project usually requiring interbusiness cooperation and sharing of resources.

Consumer credit Credit extended by a bank to a borrower for the specific purpose of financing the purchase of a household appliance, alteration, or improvement or to provide for some other personal need.

Correspondent bank A bank that is the depository for another bank. The correspondent bank accepts all deposits in the form of cash letters and collects items for its bank depositor.

Credit union A mutual thrift institution, operating under either federal or state charter, with two basic functions: promoting savings among members and providing personal loans to members at relatively low rates of interest.

Cross-selling An attempt to sell already-established customers additional services or products. In the case of financial conglomerates, cross-selling might take the form of an insurance subsidiary attempting to sell its product to the customer of a mutual fund subsidiary.

Debit card A cash machine automator and a check guarantee permitting bank customers to withdraw cash from any affiliated automated teller machine and to make cashless purchases using funds on deposit without incurring revolving financing charges for credit.

Deferred annuity An annuity contract that provides for the postponement or start of an annuity until after a specified period or until the annuitant attains a specified age.

Deintermediation Premeditated slowing of the rate of growth of bank footings, arising because banks are rapidly becoming funds brokers. The concept of allowing assets to pass through the books rather than remain on the books of banks with a fee or spread earned for initiating the transaction.

Demand deposit A sum of money placed in a bank that is payable on demand and transferable by check.

Deposit insurance Insurance to protect the depositor against bankruptcy of a bank or thrift institution.

Depository ceiling rates of interest Maximum interest rates that can be paid on savings and time deposits at federally insured banks, savings and loan associations, and credit unions. Ceilings are established by the Federal Reserve Board, the Federal Deposit Insurance Corporation, the Federal Home Loan Bank Board, and the National Credit Union Administration.

Depository institutions A financial institution that houses transaction accounts. Under the Depository Deregulation and Monetary Control Act of 1980, depository institutions include thrift institutions and commercial banks.

Depository Institutions Deregulation and Monetary Control Act (DIDMCA) Legislation passed in the spring of 1980, committing the government to deregulation of the banking system. It (1) provided for the elimination of interest rate controls for banks and savings institutions within 6 years; (2) authorized them to offer interest-bearing NOW accounts; (3) overrode many state usury ceilings on mortgage, agricultural, business, and consumer loans; (4) required the Federal Reserve to open up its discount window to all depository institutions subject to reserve requirements and to make its funds transfer payments and clearing services available to all depository institutions at the same price; and (5) gave the Federal Reserve broad new powers to control the money supply by establishing reserve requirements for all depository institutions.

Discount brokerage A brokerage firm offering commission rates on stock and bond transactions that are considerably below the commission rates charged by the established, leading brokerage firms. These firms often provide no research or advice to the customer but only execute buy and sell orders at a discount from the old fixed-rate commission structure.

Disintermediation The taking of money out of low-interest-bearing accounts at depository institutions for reinvestment at higher rates elsewhere.

Douglas Amendment to the Bank Holding Company Act of 1956 Prohibits bank holding companies from acquiring out-of-state banks unless the laws of the host state permit such entry.

Dual system of banking Refers to the fact that banks may choose to operate under either a federal or state charter.

Edge Act Corporation Subsidiaries of U.S. banks formed to permit banks to engage in international banking and financial activities. These corporations are permitted to open offices across state lines.

Electronic funds transfer systems (EFTS) A loose description of computerized systems that process financial transactions, or process information about financial transactions, or effect an exchange of value between two parties.

Endowment Life insurance payable to the policyholder if living on the maturity date stated in the policy or to a beneficiary if the policyholder dies prior to that date.

Eurodollars Deposits denominated in United States dollars and placed in banks located in such countries as the United Kingdom, the Bahamas, the Cayman Islands, and West Germany.

Federal Deposit Insurance Corporation (FDIC) A federal regulatory authority, which began operating in 1934 and which supervises banks and provides insurance protection for deposits up to $100,000. All national and state banks that are members of the Federal Reserve System are required by law to be members of the FDIC.

Federal Home Loan Bank (FHLB) One of 11 regional banks established in 1932 to encourage thrift and home financing during the Great Depression. The banks are owned jointly by various savings and loan associations. *The Federal Home Loan Bank Board* acts as its management body. The FHLB serves as a mortgage credit reserve system for home mortgage lending institutions. Members may obtain advances on home mortgages or collateral and may borrow from home loan banks under certain conditions.

Federal Reserve Bank One of 12 banks created by and operating under the Federal Reserve System. Each Federal Reserve Bank has nine directors.

Federal Reserve Board The seven member governing body of the Federal Reserve System. Appointed for 14-year terms by the President, subject to Senate confirmation, the Board has jurisdiction over bank holding companies and also sets national money and credit policy.

Federal Reserve System The title given to the central banking system of the United States as created by the Federal Reserve Act of 1913. It regulates the money supply, fixes the legal reserve of member banks, oversees the mint, effects transfers of funds, promotes and facilitates the clearance and collection of checks, examines member banks, and discharges other functions. The Federal Reserve System consists of 12 Federal Reserve Banks, their 25 branches, and the national and state banks that are members of the system.

Federal Savings and Loan Insurance Corporation (FSLIC) An organization created in 1934 for the purpose of insuring the shares and accounts of depositors up to a maximum of $100,000 of all federal savings and loan associations that apply for insurance and meet the requirements of the corporation.

Fedwire A communications network linking Federal Reserve Banks, branches, and member banks used both to transfer funds and to transmit information.

Fiduciary service A service performed by an individual or corporation acting in a trust capacity. A banking institution authorized to do a trust business may perform fiduciary services, for example, by acting as executor or administrator of an estate, as a guardian of minors, or as a trustee under wills.

Finance company Any institution other than a bank or insurance company that makes loans to business or individuals.

Financial institution An institution that uses its funds chiefly to purchase financial assets as opposed to tangible property. Financial institutions can be classified according to the nature of the principal claims they issue: nondeposit intermediaries include, among others, insurance companies, pension funds, and financial companies. Depository intermediaries obtain funds mainly by accepting deposits from the public.

Financial markets The money and capital markets of the economy. The money markets buy and sell short-term credit instruments. The capital markets buy and sell long-term credit and equity instruments.

Fixed-rate mortgage A mortgage with a fixed term, fixed rate, and fixed monthly payments.

Flexible payment mortgages An interest-only type of loan for the first 5 years. Two major restrictions apply: Each monthly payment must cover at least the interest due, and after 5 years payments must be fully amortized.

Full-service bank A commercial bank that is capable of meeting the total financial needs of the banking public.

Gensaki A repurchase agreement of a short-term nature, from a few days to a month, executed between a corporation and a Japanese brokerage firm or between a broker and a bank. Japanese money market rates are paid. The collateral is usually in the form of bonds.

Glass-Steagall Act of 1933 A legislative safeguard designed to prevent commercial banks from engaging in investment banking activities.

Grandfathered activities Nonbank activities, some of which would normally not be permissible for bank holding companies, but which were acquired or engaged in before a particular date, and may be continued under the "grandfather" clause of the Bank Holding Company Act.

Graduated-payment mortgage (GPM) A mortgage agreement in which payments are much lower at first than for traditional level payment mortgages. Payments rise gradually and level off after a few years. The idea is to put home ownership within the reach of young people who might otherwise not be able to buy because of spiraling housing prices and high interest rates. A graduated-payment adjustable mortgage combines features of the CPM and the adjustable mortgage loan authorized by the Federal Home Loan Bank Board in July 1981.

Group insurance An insurance plan under which a number of individuals and their dependents are covered by a single policy, issued to the group with which the members are affiliated, with individual certificates given to each insured person.

Growing equity mortgage (GEM) An agreement in which the interest rate is fixed for the term of the loan, but monthly payments rise with inflation. All of the increases in monthly payments are used to repay principal, shortening the maturity of the mortgage.

Guaranteed-return vehicle An agreement that promises a rate of return no matter how well or poorly an insurance company's investment portfolio performs.

Holding company A corporation that owns the securities of another, in most cases with voting control.

Homeowner's insurance A broad form of insurance coverage for real estate that combines hazard insurance with personal liability protection and other items.

Independent Bankers Association of America Created in 1930, an association to promote the interests of independent banking in the United States as a vibrant, contributing force within the economy.

Individual Retirement Account (IRA) Effective January 1, 1982, all wage earners are permitted to make tax-deductible contributions to IRAs. An individual can now save an extra $2000 a year, or a total of $2250 if there is a nonworking spouse, and let the earnings accumulate tax-free until at least age 59½.

Insurance A method whereby those concerned about some form of hazard contribute to a common fund, usually an insurance company, out of which losses sustained by the contributors are paid.

Insurance company An organization chartered under state or provisional laws to act as an insurer. In the United States, insurance companies are usually classified as fire and marine; life, property, and casualty; and surety companies. These firms may write only the kinds of insurance for which they are specifically authorized by their charters.

Investment banking The financing of the capital requirements of enterprises. The usual practice is for one or more investment bankers to buy outright from a corporation a new issue of stock or bonds. The group forms a syndicate to sell the securities to individuals and institutions. The investment banker is the underwriter of the issue.

Investment banking house One that engages in the merchandising of corporate and government securities by purchasing them in large blocks and selling them to investors. It helps to finance the capital requirements of business organizations.

Keogh plan A pension plan in which self-employed persons may set aside a portion of their yearly income in a tax-exempt account for distribution at retirement. The yearly contribution is limited to the lesser of $15,000 or 15 percent of income. The earnings on the retirement fund are not currently taxable.

Liability management The active adjustment of a financial institution's liabilities to help meet loan demand, minimize the cost of funds, and balance the maturity of liabilities with the maturity structure of assets.

Life insurance Insurance providing fixed payment of a stipulated sum to a designated beneficiary upon the death of the insured.

Macroeconomic change Changes in the aggregate economy that might be brought about by changes in government spending, taxation, interest rates, inflation, tariffs, employment, etc.

McFadden Act of 1927 Federal statute that banned interstate banking. Recently, new legislation has been proposed to encourage competition in banking by permitting interstate banking as a way to stimulate competition for consumer loans.

Member bank A commercial bank that is a member of the Federal Reserve System. All national banks are automatically members of the system, while state banks may be admitted.

Merchant banking A term used in Great Britain for an organization that underwrites securities for corporations, advises such clients on mergers, and is involved in the ownership of commercial ventures.

Monetarism A theory originated by Karl Bruner in 1968 and later expanded by James Tobin, which proposes that the money supply is the predominant influence on aggregate money income and that the quantity of money should be the target of monetary policy.

Money center banks Large commercial banks in cities such as New York, Chicago, San Francisco, and Los Angeles that are active in the money markets.

Money market fund Many investment banking firms and insurance companies sponsor money market mutual funds, which invest in short-term credit instruments. Customers earn high interest rates on the accounts and can write checks against their investment. Depository institutions were permitted to offer the equivalent of money market fund accounts in December 1982.

Mutual company A corporation without capital stock in which profits, after deductions, are distributed among the owner-customers in proportion to the business activity carried with the corporation.

Mutual fund An investment company which ordinarily stands ready to buy back its shares at their current net asset value; the value of the shares depends on the market values of the fund's portfolio securities at the time.

Mutual savings bank A banking organization without capital stock, operating under law for the mutual benefit of the depositors. The depositor is encouraged to practice thrift, and the savings of these small depositors are invested in high-grade securities and mortgages.

National bank A commercial bank organized with the consent and approval of the Comptroller of the Currency and operated under the supervision of the federal government. National banks are required to be members of the Federal Reserve System.

Nondepository institutions Financial institutions other than commercial banks, mutual savings banks, savings and loan associations, or credit unions. Insurance companies, mutual funds, pension funds, finance companies, REITs, money market funds, investment bankers, and stock brokerage firms are examples of nondepository institutions.

NOW account A savings account from which the account holder can withdraw funds by writing a negotiable order of withdrawal (NOW) payable to a third party; or (effective in 1981) an interest-bearing checking account.

Open-end investment company An investment company that sells shares to the public on a continuous basis and stands ready to redeem shares held by the public. These investment companies are often called mutual funds.

Option A right to buy (call) or sell (put) a fixed amount of a given stock at a specified price within a limited period of time. The purchaser hopes that the stock's price will go up (if he bought a call) or down (if he bought a put) by an amount sufficient to provide a profit greater than the cost of the contract and the commission and other fees required to exercise the contract. If the stock price holds steady or moves in the opposite direction, the price paid for the option is lost entirely.

Ordinary life insurance A type of insurance policy (also referred to as whole or straight life) continuing in force throughout the policyholder's lifetime and payable upon death or upon the attainment of a specified age.

Over-the-counter (OTC) (1) Securities not listed or traded on any of the regular exchanges. (2) The OTC market is one conducted by dealers throughout the country through negotiation, rather than through the use of an auction system as represented by a stock exchange.

Pass-through bonds Bonds on which monthly interest and principal less costs (mortgage servicing) are literally passed-through to the investor on a monthly basis by the issuer of the bond, who holds a pool of mortgages in portfolio for the bondholder.

Paperless item processing system (PIPS) An electronic funds transit system that is capable of performing transit functions by establishing accounting transactions by which bank funds are shifted from one ledger or subledger to another.

Pay-by-phone A service enabling customers to instruct their financial institution via telephone to initiate one or more payments from their accounts.

Point-of-sale terminal (POST) A communication and data capture terminal located where goods or services are paid for. POST terminals may save merchant accounting needs and may assist in processing financial transactions. In the latter case, the terminal may operate as part of an authorization and verification system or initiate direct exchanges of value among merchants, customers, and financial institutions.

Policy loan A loan made by a life insurance company from its general funds to a policyholder on the security of the cash value of a policy.

Portfolio A combination of investment assets, such as a group of stocks, bonds, or loans; the holdings of investments by an individual, institution, or other group.

Prime interest rate The rate of interest charged by a commercial bank for large loans made to its most creditworthy business and industrial customers; it is theoretically the lowest interest rate charged by the bank to its business customers.

Purchase money mortgage For those who put their homes on the market and find that, to sell their property, they must act as the lender themselves. The mortgage is actually a short-term instrument that runs no more than 5 years and often only a year or two. In most cases, a purchase-money mortgage is a second mortgage supplementing the buyer's partial bank financing.

Purchased money A banking term that usually refers to bank liabilities such as federal funds, repurchase agreements, large denomination certificates of deposit, Eurodollars, and other instruments where a current market rate of interest is paid for funds.

Real estate investment trust (REIT) REITs are like closed-end investment companies that specialize in construction loans, mortgages, and equity investments in real estate. The principal difference between the two is that REITs make extensive use of borrowed funds, while investment companies are not permitted to borrow funds. REITs are organized as business trusts to provide real estate portfolio management for investors who lack funds and experience and who want to maintain the liquidity that real estate investments usually do not offer.

Regulation D The regulation of the Federal Reserve Board which defines and prescribes legal reserve requirements of member banks.

Regulation Q A Federal Reserve regulation that sets a maximum interest rate that banks can pay on time and savings deposits.

Reintermediation The shift within the same depository institution from low-yielding passbook accounts to higher-yielding instruments.

Reinsurance Insurance by another insurer of all or part of a risk previously assumed by an insurance company.

Renegotiable-rate mortgage (RRM) Authorized by the Federal Home Loan Bank Board, the RRM requires home buyers to renegotiate the terms of the loan every 3 to 5 years—a distinct advantage if interest rates drop but a poor hedge against inflation if they go up.

Reserve requirements Percentage of customer deposits that banks must set aside in the form of reserves. The reserve requirement ratio determines the expansion of deposits that can be supported by each additional dollar of reserve. The board of governors of the Federal Reserve Bank can raise or lower reserve requirements for member banks within limits as specified by law.

Reverse-annuity mortgage (RAM) Designed for retirees and other fixed-income homeowners who owe little or nothing on their houses. Typically, it permits them to use some or all of the equity already in the home as supplemental income, while retaining ownership. In effect, they are borrowing against the value of the house on a monthly basis. The longer they borrow, of course, the less equity they retain in the house. The loan becomes due either on a specific date or when a specified event occurs such as the sale of the property or death of the borrower.

Revolving retail credit agreement An installment loan to an individual from a corporate retailer that is not a single-pay charge.

Savings and loan association A mutual or stock organization chartered by state or by the federal government. The association receives the savings of its members and uses these funds to finance long-term amortized mortgage loans to its members and to the general public.

Savings and Loan Holding Company Act Passed in February 1968 to provide a statutory framework for the registration, examination, and regulation of holding companies controlling one or more savings and loan associations, the accounts of which are insured by the FSLIC.

Savings bank A banking association whose purpose is to promote thrift and savings habits in a community. It may be either a stock organization or a "mutual savings bank."

Savings Bank Life Insurance (SBLI) Insurance written in several states through savings banks; characterized by having no agents selling the insurance. It is bought over-the-counter and is available in amounts limited by statute.

Securities and Exchange Commission (SEC) Established by Congress in 1934 to protect investors. The SEC administers the Securities Act of 1933, the Securities Exchange Act of 1934, the Trust Indenture Act, the Investment Company Act, and the Public Utility Holding Act. The principal provisions of these acts are: (1) The SEC administers the federal laws applying to securities. (2) Corporations issuing securities and investment bankers selling them must make full disclosure of the character of the securities. (3) Any omission of fact or insertion of false information makes all persons whose names appear on the prospectus and the registration statement liable to the purchasers of the securities for any losses suffered. (4) The organization of people, such as brokers and traders, to manipulate the price of securities is forbidden. (5) Dealings by corporation officers in securities of their own corporations are restricted. (6) The board of governors of the Federal Reserve System is given the power to fix margin requirements on loans secured by stocks and bonds.

Securities Act of 1933 Federal legislation dealing with fraud and providing for full disclosure of material facts in the issuance of securities.

Self-insurance A system whereby a firm or individual, by setting aside an amount of money, provides for the occurrence of any losses that could ordinarily be covered under an insurance program. The monies that would normally be used for premium payments are added to the special funds for payment of losses incurred. Self-insurance can be accomplished formally by the setting up of a captive insurance company by a business or by establishing high deductibles on purchased insurance by individuals.

Shared appreciation mortgage (SAM) Allows the lender of mortgage funds to share in the profit on the sale of the house in return for a lower-than-market interest rate.

Shelf registration A provision under the Securities Act of 1933 providing for the sale of securities through a prospectus. It is a method of selling securities over a period of time rather than all at one time. Corporate issuers are able to file one or more statements covering an aggregate amount of securities reasonably expected to be sold within the next two years. Once effective, the shelf prospectus can be used for single or multiple offerings through the mailing of a prospectus supplement to the SEC after the pricing of any or all of the registered securities.

Sticker supplement An adjustment made for a minor change in a shelf registration prospectus. In the past every time a corporation wished to raise additional capital in the public markets, a new prospectus had to be issued. Now, under SEC Rule 415 a company just has to place a sticker on the old prospectus with an appropriate updating of information.

Stock company (insurance) An insurance company owned by stockholders who elect a board to direct the company's management.

Society Worldwide Interbank Financial Telecommunications (SWIFT) A computer-based telecommunications system used by over 600 banks in 17 countries to reduce time and labor in processing international payments.

Surety A bond, guaranty, or other security that protects a person, corporation, or other legal entity in case of another's lack of performance, such as default in the payment of a given obligation, improper performance of a given contract, or malfeasance of office.

Surrender value Designating the amount of the total life insurance in force that will be paid to the policyholder after a certain stipulated number of premiums have been paid, if the policyholder elects to surrender the policy and receive such proportionate part. The cash surrender value of a policy is also used to determine how much will be loaned against the policy.

Swap network To finance U.S. interventions in the foreign exchange market, a series of short-term reciprocal lines between foreign banks under which the Federal Reserve System exchanges dollars for the currencies of other nations within the group, thereby allowing the Fed to buy dollars in the foreign exchange market.

Tax shelter The term applied to a means of legal avoidance of paying a portion of one's income taxes by careful interpretation of tax regulations and adjustment of one's finances to take advantage of IRS rulings.

Term insurance Life insurance payable to a beneficiary only when a policy-holder dies within a specified period. It expires without policy cash value if the insured survives the stated period.

Term loan A loan usually exceeding 1 year, but usually not more than 10 years.

Thrift institution The general term for mutual savings banks, savings and loan associations, and credit unions.

Trust (1) *General:* A fiduciary relationship between persons; one holds property for the benefit and use of another. (2) *Corporate trust:* The name applied to the division of a bank that handles the trust and agency business of corporations. (3) *Personal trust:* That branch of a trust company whose function is connected with the handling of trusts for individuals. Some of the functions performed are those of executorship of estates, administration of trust funds, investment services, and guardianship. Detailed records are maintained and statements mailed to beneficiaries of every transaction affecting a trust. (4) *Trust department:* The department of a bank that provides trust and agency services. The trust department by regulation must have books and assets separate from those of commercial banking activities.

Underwriter (1) Insurance: A company that assumes a risk for a fee. (2) Investments: An individual or party that agrees to underwrite a securities issue.

Underwriting (1) The process by which an insurance company determines whether or not it can accept an application for insurance, and if so, on what basis. (2) The process of buying all or part of a new security issue from a corporation, raising the money in the expectation that the securities can be resold to the public at a higher price.

Universal life A flexible-premium life insurance under which the policyholder may change the death benefit from time to time (with satisfactory evidence of insurability for increases) and vary the amount and timing of premium payments. Premiums (less expense charges) are credited to a policy account from which mortality charges are deducted and to which interest is credited at rates which may change from time to time.

Usury The rate of interest paid for the use of another's money, or for credit extended, which exceeds the legal limit allowed for that type of transaction by the state whose laws govern the transaction.

Variable annuity An annuity contract in which the amount of each periodic income payment may fluctuate. The fluctuation may be related to securities market values, a cost-of-living index, or some other variable factor.

Variable life insurance The death benefit is based on the performance of stocks in the insurer's portfolio. The better the market performance over the life of the policy, the more cash the benefit will receive. If the market should collapse, a specified minimum death benefit will be paid, nonetheless.

Variable-rate mortgage A type of mortgage, initially available in California, and now authorized nationally, which permits the interest charges on a loan to rise or fall automatically in accordance with a predetermined index; for instance, an index of banks' cost of funds. The interest rate can fluctuate every 6 months, but cannot be raised by more than $2\frac{1}{2}$ percentage points over the life of the mortgage. In addition, banks must offer customers a choice between variable-rate and conventional mortgages.

Whole life insurance A type of insurance policy continuing in force throughout the policyholder's lifetime and payable on his death or when he attains a specified age. The policy builds up a cash surrender value, has level premiums, and offers an option to borrow against the cash value in the policy at favorable rates. Whole life is often referred to as ordinary or straight life.

Workers' compensation A system for compensating workers injured or disabled on the job. Workers' compensation programs are established by state law and differ widely. Typically, benefits are paid under private insurance policies, but awards are determined by state boards.

Wraparound mortgages Rather than provide an entirely new mortgage at current market rates to a home buyer, the wraparound lender agrees to continue to pay the monthly installments on the existing mortgage on the home to be bought, at the original contract interest rate of the mortgage, and also to make any additional payments needed to meet the purchase price of the home.

Zero-coupon instrument A fixed income security that is offered at a substantial discount to face value. With a zero-coupon bond the investment return is the difference between the price paid for the bond and the face value at maturity. There are no coupons to clip and no periodic interest payments.

INDEX